# ARTS OF THE AMAZON

## With 192 illustrations, 148 in colour

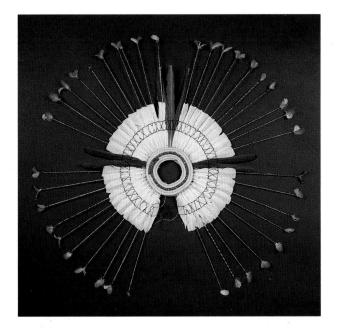

Edited by
**Barbara Braun**

Text by
**Peter G. Roe**

Preface by
**Adam Mekler**

# THAMES AND HUDSON

*Ill. p. 1*  A carved bone dagger with a bird-head pommel and fiber danglers, from the Guahibo tribe.

*Ills pp. 2–3*  *Left:*  A dorsal, concentric feather aureole headdress (*krokrokti*) from the Kayapó-Mekranoti tribe. *Right:*  A concentric feather fan headdress called an *aheto*. The Karajá wear this during the initiation ceremony for young men.

*These pages*  Two ceramic figurine compositions made by the Karajá tribe. *Left:*  Two masked male dancers facing two women perform the Aruana ceremony. *Right:*  A hunter treeing a jaguar with the aid of two dogs. While these figurines are made for sale to outsiders, similar examples are known that date to the 1800s, when they functioned as children's dolls.

© 1995 Thames and Hudson Ltd, London

British Library Cataloguing-in-Publication Data

A catalogue record for this book is available from the British Library

ISBN 0-500-27824-5

Printed and bound in Singapore

# Contents

# Preface

*This book is dedicated to my daughter Ariel Gabriella Mekler, who put up with my eccentricities and let me invade her space with the invisible people.*

As far back as I can remember, I was busy collecting objects – first stamps, then butterflies, and while still a young boy, small antiquities that were easily to be found in Israel, the country of my birth. When people refer to me as a collector, or ask me about when I started collecting, I can only reply that I really do not remember a time when I was not collecting. Ironically, I have never thought of myself as a collector in the traditional sense. One often wonders what it is that sparks the impulse to collect. I believe there are a few common traits shared by collectors such as myself, notably an insatiable curiosity, possession of a fertile imagination and an appreciation of the beautiful. The latter is of a very personal nature, since it is by definition very subjective, and will differ widely between people.

I have always loved books. While still in grammar school, I spent most of my free time in a bookstore where the proprietor agreed to let me read as much as time would allow in exchange for some dusting duties among the shelves. Needless to say, I was transported to another time, to distant lands and foreign peoples through a myriad of pages that took me away from reality to a world where I felt more at peace. It was in this fertile environment that the seeds of my fascination with the Amazon were planted.

Around 1970 I happened to watch a film on Amazonian area tribes. I was overwhelmed by the incredibly exotic and beautiful headdresses that the people were wearing. I knew immediately that I had to have these magnificent objects! Shortly thereafter, I had the opportunity to acquire my first pieces.

Initially, my interest centered around the more ornate feather headdresses, but not for long. Soon after obtaining my first pieces, an entire collection that included mostly baskets, ceramic objects, weapons, and only a few feather ornaments was offered to me. This was a turning point in my expanding interest in this material. As the collection grew, its importance and my goals became increasingly clear to me: it became imperative that these Amazonian objects, reflecting a widely unknown culture, whose people were rapidly diminishing in number, had to be taken care of and preserved. This became my mission. In order to educate myself, I began amassing a library based on every facet of the Amazon basin. Over a period of time, my knowledge about the people and their objects increased many fold.

**From left to right**

**1** A Kayapó Indian chief making a feather headdress in A-ukre village, Xingú region, eastern Brazil. The headdress this man is making (*meoko*) is worn by women during the name-giving ceremonies.

**2** A Kayabi radial feather headdress with a central diadem.

**3** An *upé* ("enemy warrior") semi-circular, wooden trophy-head mask made by the Tapirapé tribe. It is adorned with blue, yellow and scarlet macaw and parrot feathers.

**4–6** Asurini painted jars used for liquid foods. They have a post-fire resin crust.

Amazing as it may seem, considering the recent interest and exposure given to the rainforest and its destruction, very little attention has been paid to the people of the Amazon and their culture. While the art of other non-Western cultures – African, Oceanic, North-American Indian, Eskimo, and Asian – has been studied extensively, the disregard shown for Amazonian tribal art is inexcusable. The aesthetic value of the art forms created by the Indians of the Amazon basin is comparable to that of all other cultures of the world, yet their creations are often referred to as anthropological objects rather than as works of art. Could it be because we in Western culture still cling to the assumption that before an object can be considererd a work of art it must first be assigned a monetary value? I find it very disappointing that in most of the anthropological literature concerning the various tribes, there is seldom a photograph or a mention of any of their artistic creations. This total lack of recognition deprives these people of their humanity as expressed through their art. Authors have unjustly characterized the Amazonian people as savage, fierce, and primitive. One wonders whether these descriptions are but a reflection on our own culture and the devastation that we have wrought upon

these people since our first encounter with them in the 16th century. It is my hope that this publication will help to dispel some of the distorted views we have about the Amazonian people, their art and their culture.

This book has its roots in one of the first exhibitions about Amazonian art presented in the United States, which was at the Fresno Art Museum, California, and was followed shortly thereafter by a second exhibition sponsored by the Bowers Museum of Cultural Art in Santa Ana, California.

I wish to thank a few special people who had the foresight to exhibit these objects as works of art rather than as anthropological curiosities, especially Robert Barrett, Director of the Fresno Art Museum, Mimi and Bernie West, George and LaVona Blair, and David S. Yamaguchi for making the first effort possible; also E.Z. Smith for his photography, Barbara Braun for her heroic efforts as editor and coordinator, Peter Roe for his scholarly essay, Michael Bernstein for his advice, Russell A. Mittermeier for his contribution, Paul Apodaca, curator of the Bowers Museum, for the use of their Amazonian photographs, and Daphne Beneke for her support, understanding and assistance.
*Adam Mekler, 1994*

7 Wayana men preparing *orok* headdresses for the ant-shield ceremony, the Tocandira, in the village plaza, Surinam.

*Opposite:* **10 Known as an *orok* by its Wayana-Aparai creators, this tall, cylindrical basketry feather headdress-body dance costume is the most complex one in their inventory, and is also employed in the ant-shield ceremony. Covered with feather mosaic, it has feather projections ending in beetle wing casings and palm-raffia danglers.**

**8 A ceremonial feather mosaic pectoral (*kupixi*) used in the Wayana-Aparai ant-shield ceremony, made from plaited split cane, beeswax, red *urucu* and black *genipa* paints, and white clay. Its regularly overlapping feathers replicate the breast feathers of a bird; the central motif is a stylized jaguar. Wearing this pectoral, together with a feathered headdress and feathered arm ligatures, the male dancer is transformed into a bird.**

**9 A Wayana-Aparai feather flute mask (*rueimon*). The feathers are from the scarlet macaw and the frame is cotton and fiber. A pan flute hangs behind this large mask.**

To think about the Amazon today is to embrace the profound tension between the forces of destruction and preservation at work there. It is one of the world's richest biological regions, encompassing the rainforests of northeastern South America and the cultures of approximately 120 once-isolated Indian tribes, and spanning eight modern nations. While it has been exploited by white adventurers since the 16th-century Conquest of the Americas, economic development and the consequent despoilation of its human, animal, vegetable and mineral resources have intensified in the past decade. Almost daily, news reports detail fresh assaults to the rainforest ecology and onslaughts on the lifeways of its indigenous inhabitants as encroaching industries such as oil, mining, logging and ranching and expanding populations bring pollution to major rivers, soil depletion and deforestation. At the same time, the various ethnic groups inhabiting the rainforest are threatened by poverty, malnutrition, disease, bloodshed, cultural extinction and despair. Five hundred years after the European Conquest, fewer than 200,000 Indians remain in the region, out of a population estimated at 3.5 million at the turn of the century.

The terrible plight of Brazil's Yanomamö Indians, a group of 6–9,000 individuals, is one well-documented example of this process. Basically warriors who live by hunting and gathering and by limited cultivation, they occupy the frontier area of Brazilian expansion, along the upper Río Negro near the Venezuelan border. In the 1980s one of the world's richest deposits of gold and diamonds was discovered in their remote territory. The ensuing gold rush has brought thousands of miners and prospectors who have destroyed the rainforest, polluted the streams with mercury, introduced deadly malaria, and provoked and brutally attacked the Indians.

The miners who recently entered a Yanomamö village and massacred seventy unarmed men, women and children may have viewed these Indians' bellicosity as evidence of their "savagery," and taken this as license to kill them.

Moral outrage and a heightened awareness of the irreplaceable riches that are being lost in the Amazon have generated a groundswell of international resistance to such devastation. More and more, scientists are recognizing the importance of the rainforest to the biological health of the entire planet. They understand that the inhabitants of the jungle have much to teach the modern world about living in a balanced relationship with the ecosystem, about the medicinal uses of plants and about the practical aspects of surviving in a difficult environment. The Kayapó of northern Brazil, for example, cultivate dozens of plants that grow together harmoniously, domesticate and classify insects, employ biological pest control and practice a complex form of medicine, taking advantage of virtually everything that grows around their villages.

Strenuous efforts, on the part of many outside advocacy groups and the Indians themselves through self-help associations, are underway to counteract this devastation by protecting the rainforest environment and preserving the indigenous culture. Inevitably, however, industrial development proceeds apace and the surviving Indians of the Amazon are becoming acculturated to white society. Yet they are not all about to disappear or become extinct, as is commonly supposed. Instead, two kinds of adaptation are taking place. Those Indian groups who abandon their cultural heritage and passively enter the nation state, adopting Western clothing styles, language and customs, invariably become absorbed into the white culture on the lowest level – as day laborers and servants. They also become dependent

# The Amazon Today

*Opposite:* **11 A Kamayurá Indian man in full regalia, dressed for the Javari ceremony. He is wearing the typical Xinguano feathered ear tubes and a feathered crown headdress.**

*Below:* **12 A Yanomamö Indian man in ceremonial attire, assuming the warrior's pose. He sports the traditional bowl-cut coiffure, wears feathered upper-arm ligatures and a breech cloth made from imported trade cloth, and holds a quid of tobacco under his lower lip.**

13 A macaw-feather crown with danglers, made by the Kayapó-Kreen Akrore.

*Below:* 14 A radial parrot-feather headdress (*menoko*) from the Kayapó-Txukahamae tribe, with a central diadem of scarlet macaw plumes.

*Opposite*

15 A Waiapi cane head-band (*akaneta*), adorned with small, regularly overlapping toucan feathers and a blue-breasted *cotinga* bird pelt dangler.

16 A fiber headband adorned with small, regularly overlapping toucan feathers and parrot feather danglers, made by the Piaroa tribe.

on showy new Western gadgets and locked into the corporate culture that produces them, at the expense of ties to their kinspeople.

Those groups that have been able to sustain themselves with their ethnic identity intact have developed a different, more dynamic strategy of accommodation to the dominant socio-economic system. Many of them have been in contact with white society for a long time, including the Shipibo of the Peruvian *montaña*, the Yekuana of Venezuela, the Canelos Quichua of Ecuador and the Tukuna on the crossroads of Brazil, Colombia and Peru. They have also repeatedly experienced waves of foreign intrusion and abuse over the past 150–200 years – missionaries, the rubber boom of the late 19th–early 20th century, the discovery of petroleum – and have survived. The Kayapó, for example, who live, like the Yanomamö, in mining and lumber territory in the expanding Brazilian frontier, actively participate in many facets of the contemporary world, including the cash economy, and manage to stay on good terms with their white neighbors without compromising their sociocultural integrity.

To a great extent they accomplish this through their art-making, which is intimately linked with rituals and ceremonies such as initiation and funerary rites, shamanic practices and social visiting. Researchers have shown that those Indian groups who continue to make multiple references to their ethnic identity in art and rituals preserve their integrity and survive as a part of the multicultural world. Distinctive ornaments and unique styles expressing the group's own symbolism and meaning, which are inspired by ancient Indian culture, cosmology, mythology, and ecological knowledge, help maintain their power structure and reaffirm cultural and linguistic traditions.

At the same time as many of these groups make inwardly directed art for their own use, they often produce a different kind of art for the ethnic arts market – unfairly derided as "airport art" – with which they augment their incomes. Art designed for external consumption provides these Indians with a measure of financial independence in a cash economy and enables them to exercise some power over their own lives.

The arts of the Amazon are characterized by a similar tension between the forces of destruction and preservation that underscores the crisis of the rainforest. Most of the artifacts, except for ceramics, are made out of perishable materials – wood, cloth, fiber, feathers – and destined to be reabsorbed into the rainforest environment after a short life. Were it not for preservation by collectors and museums of anthropology and art, a good deal of this ephemeral beauty and cultural richness would have disappeared. While originally intended to be functional and transient, these objects may be said to have become functionless and fixed in their new contexts. But their preservation has allowed anthropologists and art historians to derive new meaning about the complex system of beliefs, knowledge and social organization of the societies that made them – and about human experience in general, especially that of a balanced relation between people and their environment. Moreover, because these objects often carry on the patterns established by their makers' ancient ancestors, they can also provide insights into prehispanic culture, despite drastic disjunctions since the 16th century. As a matter of fact, Amazonian Indians themselves are now making their own museums to preserve their art.

Adam Mekler, a West-Coast collector with a passionate devotion to the arts of the Amazon, has assembled the largest and probably the finest private collection of this material in the United States, comparable in quality to the holdings of the American Museum of Natural History, New York, the Field Museum, Chicago, and the University of Pennsylvania Museum, Philadelphia. Acquired over the past two decades, the collection encompasses over one thousand items, including hundreds of featherworks, masks, headdresses, full-body costumes, wooden, ceramic, woven and mixed-media objects from over eighty tribes. In the process Mekler has become a scholar of Amazonian arts, carefully documenting the cultural provenience and significance of each object, and has bent his every effort towards their preservation and dissemination.

Mekler's approach to the material is an unabashedly aesthetic one; he believes that the beauty and the craftsmanship embodied in certain of these objects are the equivalent of Western art and should be acknowledged as such. Though most early observers admired the intricate skill and craftsmanship with which these objects were made, they have traditionally been regarded as curiosities of an exotic New World and, later, as anthropological specimens, rather than as aesthetic achievements. Mekler is particularly drawn to the variety of ceremonial objects – regalia and body ornaments of all kinds – fashioned from or decorated with the brilliant plumage of tropical birds: headdresses, dance costumes, necklaces, armbands, ear and nose ornaments, pendants, artifacts used in rituals. Among his most treasured possessions is a complete representation of the featherwork objects used in the important Tocandira initiation ritual of the Wayana-Aparai, including the headdress and body costume, plaited plaque covered with macaw and parrot feathers, shaman's scepter, chest ornament holding the fire ants that the initiates are exposed to, and an extremely rare flute mask. Other spectacular feather-works in the collection are several Tapirapé

masks and headdresses and body ornaments made by the Karajá, Kayapó, Kamayurá, Tukuna, Urubú-Kaapor and Waiwai tribes.

While heavily weighted in favor of featherworks, nearly half of the collection consists of ceramics, carved wooden and mixed-media objects. Important ceremonial items include huge Shipibo-Conibo decorated ceramic vessels and male and female figurines made by the Karajá tribe; wax, wood and shell masks; woven garments; and dance and ritual costumes, including the extremely rare full-body costume worn by the shaman in the Uvat curing ritual practiced by the Xingú-Kamayurá. There are also ceremonial necklaces, pendants, combs, ear ornaments, rattles, and wooden stools from various tribes. Although some practical everyday objects – weapons, implements, containers and storage vessels – are represented in the collection, Mekler is less interested in the mundane and utilitarian; there are, for example, very few items relating to bellicose activites, and no toys, traps or tree-climbing sticks.

In favoring the ceremonial featherwork artistry of the Amazon, Mekler continues a long tradition going back to the first contacts between the European and native American worlds. From that moment on, featherworks have been among the most prized Indian artifacts. As the art historian Hugh Honour has pointed out, it was of all the living creatures the birds of the West Indies and South America that most impressed the early explorers, especially parrots, macaws and toucans, which epitomized the brilliance and beauty of nature in the New World. Christopher Columbus mentioned parrots in his first letter and brought them back to Europe in 1493; Brazil was often called the land of the parrots in the early 1500s; and America was mainly represented by featherwork in European cabinets of natural and artificial curiosities. The extraordinary feather

*Below:* **17 A pair of wooden ear pins adorned with toucan feathers, from the Kuikúru tribe.**

*Bottom:* **18 This twill-weave ant and wasp glove is modeled after a stingray and has projecting scarlet macaw feathers. It is used during the Waiamiri-Atroari initiation ceremonies for young men.**

headdress that was bestowed on Hernán Cortés by Moctezuma, and thought to be the latter's own, was preserved in a princely cabinet of curiosity and is now a centerpiece of the anthropology museum in Vienna.

Gaily colored birds have also played a prominent part in Western visual images of America. Alexander Humboldt, one of the first scientifically trained Europeans to extensively explore the South-American rainforest, conveyed the conventional 18th-century view in his magnum opus about America: "When we speak in Europe of a native of Guiana... we figure to ourselves a man whose head and waist are decorated with the fine feathers of the macaw, the toucan and the humming bird. Our painters and sculptors have long since regarded these ornaments as the characteristic marks of an American."

Though Mekler departs from earlier enthusiasts in his aesthetic appreciation of Amazonian material, in his higher valuation of Indian ceremonial regalia over everyday utensils and tools he is thoroughly traditional. Anthropologist Peter Roe's fascinating essay in this volume might be said to correct this quintessentially Western bias by acknowledging the importance of ceremonial and utilitarian artifacts alike – to give us a more comprehensive picture of all Amazonian artifacts and their cultural context. Drawing on his extensive fieldwork among the Shipibo-Conibo and the Cariban Waiwai Indians, respectively living on the southwestern edge and the northeastern rim of the vast Amazon basin, and on his special ethnographic interest in the visual, verbal and performative arts, as well as the cosmology and astronomy of the Amazon, Roe explains how all of these objects are bearers of meaning and are fully integrated into the lives of their makers. He also shows us that every aspect of the arts of the Amazon involves a process of creative transformation, including beliefs surrounding the gathering and preparation of materials, sets of symbols, design, technique and function, and that each of these aspects recapitulates the messages incorporated in the others.

As a trained archaeologist, Roe also evokes the cultural continuity between present-day populations and their ancestors and reminds us that the traditions of feather ornamentation, ceramic-making and weaving extended very far back in time in the Central and Northern Andes. The miraculously preserved exquisite feather mosaics on cloths and body ornaments of ancient Peru recovered from archaeological sites, as well as the feather ornaments in the iconography of north- and south-coast ceramics, textiles and gold masks, can be provocatively compared with contemporary ethnographic examples from the Amazon region. A feather headdress worn by a Chimu chieftain depicted on a feather mosaic panel, for instance, or one excavated at the site of Caudivilla in the Chillon Valley closely resemble those worn by present-day Amazon Indians. Even more profoundly, by making clear the kinetic and performative aspects of these artifacts in their Amazonian cultural context, Roe suggests different perspectives that might be helpful in understanding enigmatic archaeological material, and he reminds us that we need to look for similarities as well as differences between modern and ancient inhabitants of the Americas, even in prehispanic cultures with urban dimensions and monumental forms.

Surely the best way to preserve the culture of the Amazon is through a cultural explication of indigenous artifacts coupled with an aesthetic appreciation and wonderment – asserting that these artifacts are documents of unwritten knowledge as well as beauty. It is our hope that this volume contributes to that process.

*Barbara Braun, 1994*

# Arts of the Amazon

## The Jungle Setting

The vast, but imperilled, Amazonian jungle is an overwhelming place. It is a dark, green, leafy world encompassing an overabundance of life and the certainty of death. Everything is either in riotous growth or in equally rapid decomposition as the rainforest recycles itself ceaselessly.[1] It is a place of awesome beauty as well as of danger and discomfort, from the oppressive humidity and the vines and thorns that rip at one's flesh to the myriad mosquitoes, chiggers, leaches and other life forms that feed on the errant traveler. Larger threats, such as vipers, boas, caimans and jaguars, are now scarce, except in the remotest of regions, as a result of merciless exploitation.

One never feels more alive than walking through the funereal gloom of the forest floor – a land of shadows suddenly pierced by slanting columns of bright light filtering through the canopy high above – or sitting in the prow of a canoe, gazing at the wall of tangled and towering growth spawned where the sun reaches the ground along the river banks. Pungent smells of bloom and decay fill the air, and sounds, strange and undefinable, echo from the sun-drenched world 200 feet above one's head. At night the stage shrinks to the empty space of a village's cleared plaza ringed by a wall of dark vegetation. Above is a crystal-clear black sky speckled with a vast profusion of strange southern-hemisphere stars and the running river of the Milky Way, all nearly invisible in the hazy and light-polluted northern skies.

## Canoe Indians and Foot Indians

Two broad types of human adaptation characterize these humid lowlands. The first is that of the Canoe Indians who live along the muddy, meandering broad rivers of the Amazon and adjacent basins, like the Orinoco to the north. These riverine populations are at home on the water, paddle about in dugout canoes and fish for the abundant aquatic protein in the rivers and the annually flooded rainforest bordering it. This is a complex watery landscape of interconnected rivers, paralleling natural levees, backswamps and isolated oxbow lakes,[2] and on the high ground bordering the floodplain large, long, and narrow villages of Indians thrive. They are experts in the creation of elaborate polychrome pottery. One such society is the numerous Panoan-speaking Shipibo-Conibo of the Peruvian *montaña* on the southwestern edge of the vast Amazon basin. Another is the Aruak-speaking Waurá of the Xingú culture area.

The Foot Indians of the interior, the other major adaptation to the lowlands, forage as nomads or use an extensive form of slash-and-burn horticulture. They live in small circular villages in the old, heavily leached and well-drained alluvial soil of the mature tropical rainforest, or they frequent the natural savannahs that intrude upon it in certain regions. They are expert woodsmen and the supreme hunters of the forest fauna of monkeys and birds. Their technology is characterized by lightweight and flexible basketry, and they form either bands or tribes. The Foot Indians are thinly spread over the land of the interfluves. One society exemplifying this niche is the Cariban Waiwai of Guyana and Brazil, forest denizens of the northeastern rim of the Amazon basin.[3] The Gê groups of the major southern tributaries of the Lower Amazon form a second type of seasonal foragers-and-farmers. Along with the Bororo, they represent an ancient people inhabiting the scrub and savannah landscape of the Brazilian shield, residing in large and complexly organized wheel-shaped villages in the wet season. Here they enjoy a rich ceremonial life, and then break up into band-sized units for trekking into the hinterland during the dry season.

19 A pair of toucan-feather cane ear tubes made by the Yawalapití tribe.

*Below:* 20 A Kuikúru jaguar-claw necklace. A man must earn the right to wear it by demonstrating valor, certain personal attributes and social position.

Representative groups from this adaptation are the Gê-speaking Kayapó who sport lower lip discs and a sub-tribe, recently contacted, the Txukahamae.

## The Mists of Prehistory

These contrasting adaptations have been refined over many millennia. Nevertheless, until the 1970s the archaeology of the lowlands of South America was in thrall to a Green Hell vision of an unproductive jungle unable to sustain the emergence of complex social life and civilization. It was depicted by some North-American archaeologists as an undifferentiated zone of low-density tribal and band populations living a rudimentary slash-and-burn village horticultural way of life.[4] Dense populations were supposedly limited by the lack of large animals to hunt in the jungle. All complex culture was thought to be late, derived from the highlands and coast of the great South American civilizations of Peru, the Colombian and Venezuelan Andes (or sometimes even from shipwrecked Jomon Japanese fishermen). Lastly, this position maintained that even if such highland-derived cultures entered the lowlands, they did so late in time and were destined to "devolve" once they were unhappily ensconced in the Amazon. This bleak vision of the contribution of the lowlands to South American culture history is attributable to ethnographic contact with the Waiwai in the less-productive Guianan highlands, where settlement size is, in fact, small (less than fifty people per village) and was influenced by the poor preservation of artifacts in the jungle compared to the excellent preservation characteristic of the arid lands bordering the Amazon to the west. Of course, the fact that little archaeological evidence remains in the steamy jungle does not mean that dense and precocious populations did not exist there – but that most of their material culture was made out of the same perishable organic materials as the rainforest itself. That preservational bias and the use of faulty field and analytical techniques yielded erroneous lowland chronologies and hence an incorrect picture of coastal precosity and lowland marginality. In effect, this reconstruction missed the Canoe Indian completely and focused only on the Foot Indians of the interior – the peoples who had, precisely because of their small village size and backwoods placement, escaped the scythe of initial European contact, warfare and disease.

Yet evidence existed in the 16th-century reports of Dominican friar Gaspar de Caravajal, chronicler of the brilliant Spanish explorer Francisco de Orellana,[5] that belied such a bleak vision of lowland culture history. Orellana was the first white man to descend the entire length of the Amazon from the highlands of Ecuador to the Atlantic coast, passing (at times eventfully) through dense, complex human societies on the main river along the way. These numerous and warlike groups ranged from the large-scale chiefdoms of the Omagua on the Upper Amazon, near its western tributaries, to what was very probably the emergent mini-state of the Tapajós on the Lower Amazon. But because Europeans first entered the lowlands by these same watery routes inhabited by these impressive societies, they were the first to disappear as victims of "civilization." So early did they vaporize that their bellicose achievements and the remains of the antecedent Marajoara civilization have only recently emerged through the work on Marajó island and its environs.[6]

This archaeological record indicates that the current ethnographic literature based on studies of recently pacified and pitiable remnants of "tribal isolates" is, in fact, a profoundly misleading guide to lowland pre-contact social organization and behavior, particularly with regard to the role of warfare and raiding, which were endemic in pre-contact times yet are now virtually nonexistent. Extant societies do prove a reliable introduction to lowland religion and cosmology, however, because those domains are infinitely more conservative than social organization or even ecological orientation. The far-ranging population movements and contacts between groups along the waterways, and all the way out into the Caribbean, attested to by the archaeological finds, and the complexity and bellicosity described in the ethnohistoric documents, have all vanished from the literature. The result is a well-meaning presentation of Indians as peace-loving, egalitarian and docile, mere victims of white aggression. While victims they manifestly are, to depict lowlanders in only their pacified current state without acknowledging the violent past robs them of a measure of their own humanity. We do not see these groups for what they are, the reconstituted remnants of much larger, more sophisticated and warlike lowlanders who actively contributed a whole series of cultigens and cultural practices to all civilizations, highland and lowland, in South America, long before the coming of Europeans.

This view began to change with the publication of Donald Lathrap's *The Upper Amazon* in 1970, which argued that the lowlands along the main rivers of South America were a prime environment for the evolution of culture, like the Nile Delta. Fertile soils deposited by annual floods permitted intensive agriculture yielding high-protein nutrients, like corn, while at the same time, extensive slash-and-burn plots of carbohydrate-yielding crops like manioc could be maintained on the surrounding higher bluffs that were not inundated.[7] Moreover, these two types of agriculture could have been complemented by the secure animal protein found in the rivers. Just one of the tributaries of the

Amazon, for example, can yield more species of fish than all the temperate rivers of North America and Europe combined![8] Thus, dense human populations could arise there at a very early time, leading to the documented pattern of widespread migration and critical technical inventions like pottery and loomed textiles.

Lathrap's vision has been corroborated in the intervening years. We now know, for example, that the prehistory of lowland societies stretches back to the late Ice Age, when humans first entered its humid realm. Cave sites in the southern Brazilian highlands and the Chilean coastal site of Monte Verde point to the possibility of generalized hunter-and-gatherer settlements as early as 25–30,000 B.C. Recent secure dating of paint splatter on ancient living floors from cave pictographs in the Lower Amazon place riverine foraging as early as 15,000 B.C. and even document the first invention of pottery in the New World by riverine foragers by 7000 B.C., long before secure horticulture ever existed. In fact, Lathrap and his North-American and Ecuadorian students have shown how lowland innovations like pottery, loomed textiles, and complex zoomorphic religious imagery backed by hallucinatory shamanism intruded into northern Peru from southern Ecuador – all phenomena with Amazonian roots.[9]

## The Animating Spirit

The evergreen jungle and the broad, muddy rivers of the lowlands form the natural contexts for all the ancient arts and crafts and surviving expressions to be seen in the pages of this book. Probably the best way to approach these artifacts is to view them in terms of two major metaphors – animism and gender. The first is that they comprise an animistic material culture; they are items that are wrested from nature with but the slightest modification and made to serve as

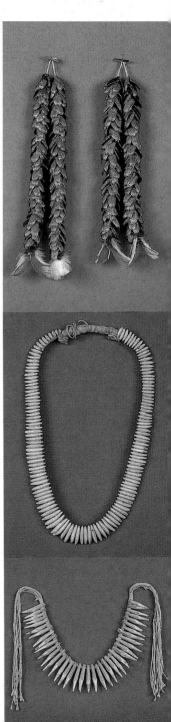

21 A pair of iridescent green beetle wing casing ear danglers, made by the Aguaruna.

22 A Kayapó-Txukahamae necklace of monkey teeth, which have been abraded to make them uniform.

23 A Kayapó-Mekranoti animal-tooth necklace.

**Top: 24** A Bororo peccary-tusk necklace. The tusks are held together with wax.

**25** A Bora ocelot-skull necklace with seeds and feathers, worn only by shamans.

human technology. The second focuses on whether it is men or women who create and use the objects.

A canine pried from a peccary's mandible and employed as a scraper, a freshwater mussel shell perforated and used as tweezers, a plume plucked from the tail of a bird and tied to a headdress frame are all examples of the "animated" transformations of natural forms into artifacts that are made possible by the profusion of raw materials in the forest and the waters that inundate it. Iridescent beetle wing casings, fish's bony tongues, snake ribs, animal claws, teeth, skulls, variegated and spectacularly tinted bird plumes, turtle carapaces, freshwater shells, rich woods, strong vines and shiny leaves all comprise these ephemeral artifacts, destined to rot within a few years back into the forest whence they came.

As natural objects, these are infused with the ideology of animism, a belief in the total spirituality of the universe. This world view informs all lowland South-American Indian cultures. It maintains that everything that grows, moves or develops must, like humans, have a soul. All over the lowlands this view is reinforced by the spiritual transformations of man into beast or bird via the ingestion of hallucinogenic drugs and the curing-bewitching shamanism that derives from this same world view.[10]

Such tropical animism engenders a very different attitude toward nature from the West's fixation on control and domination. In the jungle a prayer of forgiveness is uttered when an animal like a sloth is killed to render up its hide for a drum head or an eagle captured to yield its down and feathers for a headdress. Only that which is needed is killed, otherwise the Masters and Mistresses of the game species (the large "platonic" prototypes of the species) will become angry and not let their children be taken by ungrateful human hunters.[11] Since nature is the source of the raw materials that comprise

the artifacts, the shape and format of artifacts also emulate nature. Most artifacts are ephemeral, made for one-time use only and then thrown away to recycle like leaf detritus back into the forest, or they are called into being as the need arises and discarded once it is satisfied; for those artifacts that are made from more permanent materials, reuse is another way to recycle resources and effort. A Waiwai burden basket, for example, is woven in five minutes from two palm fronds to carry balls of potting clay from a forest rivulet and is discarded once the village is reached. A cut-down tree becomes an impromptu bench, or a worn-out wooden canoe turns into a grinding mortar. Huts are organic constructions, virtually bare of possessions, and those that do exist are invisibly stuck into the thatch above one's head. Yet those few objects are often exquisitely and ingeniously made, with considerable decoration.

Tropical forest peoples consider that an artifact must be decorated, with either geometric or representational designs, for it to be complete.[12] Our own cultural bias towards undecorated utilitarian objects contrasts sharply with this notion. A second aspect of "animistic technology" dictates that all artifacts, rather than being credited to individual inventors (the heroes of Western history), are captured in South-Amerindian thought from animal and plant "donors." In mythic time they held all the designs, but they did so *naturally*, in the patterning of their scales, the markings on their pelts, or the veining in their leaves. Moreover, the shape and behavior of these animal and plant donors explain the very form and function of the artifact. The designs on twill-weave baskets came from the patterned hide of the anaconda "Dragon"; the painted designs on textiles or pottery imitate the intricate quatrefoil spots of the jaguar; the way a manioc-squeezing basketry tube first thickens and then lengthens is likened to the devouring anaconda; the fire-fan fell to earth as a freshwater ray and turned into the artifact of that shape.[13]

These stories of creation place the origin of each artifact in the natural world, and thus deflect one's focus from their human creators to the stolen "talents" of animals, plants and birds. Thus behind each artifact is a myth, and each myth in turn refers to artifacts. This pattern of "mutual referentiality" was first noted by the Danish ethnographer Niels Fock while working among the Waiwai.[14] While academic specialists in the West divide these genres into different disciplines like folklore and anthropology, the creators of the stories and the objects to which they refer do not. All arts, all media are interconnected in the ceremonial or ritual performance. Music, dance, artifacts and accoutrements together sing the praises of the animals or assert temporary dominance over them. For contrary to our own world view, which holds that humans evolved from favored animals, thereby establishing the mental and physical rubicons dividing "us" from "them," the Indians look back to "were-creatures," neither animal nor human, which devolved into animals through moral failings. Peccaries were once people who didn't obey the incest rules and turned into wild pigs. Indians see them as our misguided cousins, and consider that we could be like them if we did not adhere to our customs. Thus when we kill them for meat or to extract their incisors to use as tools, we convert them back from nature into culture. In the same way we "civilize" to death a human enemy and turn his frontal bone into a carved and decorated pectoral which we wear, or we turn his severed head into an adorned trophy to simultaneously confirm domination over him and to absorb his vital force.[15] When we take his women and turn them into proper brides, the speakers of our language and the bearers of our children, we "rescue" them from a life little better than that of the beasts.[16]

## Art, Artifact and Western Myopia

Until recently the impressive objects produced by this world view were under-appreciated and little known. Unfortunately, these organic collages of feathers, seeds, hair, beetle wing cases, animal teeth and claws, gourds and vines, no matter how visually and kinetically expressive, did not coincide with traditional Western notions of what constituted art. Euro-Americans have always preferred a medium-based definition of art; it should be composed of the precious (gold, silver, gems) or the monumental (bronze, marble) and it should be static, fixed and useless. In short, if it wasn't a statue of bronze or marble, or a painting in oils with an ornate frame, it wasn't art. Even the Impressionist, Cubist and Expressionist revolutions in the recent history of modern Western art, the same revolutions that opened the tradition to both Oriental and African art, left largely untouched the contributions of the American Indian. Partly this was because the material culture of these civilizations had either a preciousness (Oriental) or a monumentality (three-dimensional wood sculpture or bronze bas-reliefs) that fulfilled Western notions of the true art object, however barbaric or inscrutable. With the exception of the similarly monumental and sculptural art of ancient Mesoamerican or Peruvian civiliz-ations, or possibly the substantial wooden creations of the Amerindian cultures of the Pacific Northwest Coast, the artifacts of Native Americans have been considered mere ethnological curios, suitable for display along with fossil dinosaurs or stuffed bears in museums of natural history, but not worthy of exhibition in art museums.

For these reasons, the rich and incredibly beautiful, yet evanescent, arts of the

Amazonian jungle – neither monumental, static, fixed nor useless – have languished outside of the Western aesthetic consciousness. Adam Mekler's peerless and meticulously documented collection of Amazonian arts will help redress our Eurocentric bias by revealing to us a world of great and threatened beauty. Perhaps we may even be energized to demand its better preservation in countless dank museum sub-basements where so much of it now languishes, as well in the jungles where it is still being created.

### Theme and Variations in Ethnic Art

Lowland artifacts of the Amazon convey an overwhelming impression of tremendous vitality and creativity, especially when seen in the context of the performances they embellish. As in more familiar European folk societies, that creativity is often expressed by a "theme and variations" approach. That is, the culture – or more specifically various "audiences" within it – set the general theme, the artist spins endless variations on these themes, testing his/her ingenuity to both fulfill and stretch the limits of traditional styles. It is important for the artist to be original, but not too original, to stay within the canons of the style, but also to experiment – and thus satisfy both the artist's and the audience's desires for novelty. For, in the jungle, where modern cultural geographers have documented it takes only about three and one-half hours a day to do all one has to do for food, clothing and shelter,[17] the problem is not drudgery but boredom. In these original leisure societies, art becomes both a pleasant pastime and an enjoyable feast for the eyes. It is everywhere, and its ubiquitousness explains the very absence of terms such as "art" or "artist." One only needs words for this process in cultures like our own, where the creator and his/her creation are segregated from daily life, consigned to the

art ghetto of galleries or museums. Pervasive lowland creativity was simply overlooked. Anthropologists often took at face value Indians' assertions that they never "invent" anything, but rather copy everything from the ancients. An anonymous Makiritare (Yekuana) Indian has been quoted as saying, "It's always the same, now as before. The way we ate once, we do over and over again. We obey. We remember. The old ones sing beautifully. We just repeat."[18] In a similar way the Shipibo affirm that some of their designs were copied from the pelt of the giant anaconda Dragon, while others were given to them by their culture-hero Inca ancestors.[19]

Such assertions do not mean that traditional artists fail to innovate; they do so, and constantly, in everything from novel songs[20] and new spirits to original myths and creative designs. What these statements mean is that in small face-to-face societies artists can never admit that they do so. Instead, the anthropologist or visitor gets the official ideology of continuity with the mythic past, *not* what is actually happening in the everyday present. That is why [s]he must always observe and not merely question.

There are other reasons why individual creators cannot parade their creativity. One anthropologist cites the case of a Waurá artist from the Xingú who created a whole new genre by drawing representational animals, spirits and men, using crayons supplied him. The tribal style was geometric patterning. He hid his drawing for the several months it took him to create his fascinating menagerie, fearing that he would be accused of witchcraft by his fellow villagers. In the lowlands, to draw an outline in the sand of the plaza is tantamount to creating a real being, in myth as in life. Such societies also clothe individuals in a "social mask" of compulsory pleasantness. Whether they paint their faces in a delicate tracery of organic dyes or merely affect impassive visages, lowland tribal people are members of "mask cultures," as the French anthropologist Claude Lévi-Strauss first observed among the Mbayá-Caduveo of the Gran Chaco to the south.[21] But even as people feign indifference to slights, secret witchcraft abounds. And periodically, via the mechanism of "pattern drunkenness" in the impressive manioc beer festivals, these tensions explode in violent confrontation. Then, as the village is littered with pools of blood and torn hair, the recovering population resumes its impassive ways until the next fiesta. It would appear, therefore, that the Waurá artist's fears were justified.

Artists protect themselves from the inevitable indirect comments about their egotism by avoiding undue assertions of individual authorship. In accord with the principle of "indirect ascription," the artist deflects interest from him/herself by referring such creation to the ancestors or the animal "spirit donors" of the art. Not only does this confer ancestral and religious legitimacy upon personal creativity, it also removes the loci of interest from the imperfect present of the conflicted self to the remote, mythic, and hence perfect, past of the ancestors.

This flight from egotism is characteristic of South Amerindians, where deference to others and effacement of self are important social characteristics. The anti-social person is one who is egotistical, such egotism becoming a symbol of social atomism and the destruction of culture. The same holds for aesthetics. Thus, while the Cashinahua Indians of the Peruvian *montaña* admire the *tour de force* of the master craftswoman,[22] they harshly criticize anyone who *overreaches*, that is, tries to achieve too complicated a vision for her limited technical attainments.[23] Such a person fails by a public demonstration of hubris as much as by a lack of skill. This phenomenon explains the common South-Amerindian cultural pattern of watching, but not trying to practice (at least in public), a skill or an art before it has been mastered. It also explains why verbal instruction and active questioning are rare in the learning of skills. Instead, close observation is coupled with detailed repetitive mastery of motor control.

These mechanisms of modesty and reticence fit with what a student of the Kayapó calls the distinction between social and mythic agency.[24] Societies lodged in history, such as our own, attribute creation to unique individuals like those who are alive today, thereby affirming the personal ability actively to produce and reproduce culture in the present and future. In contrast, societies which exist without history passively attribute creation to the spirits or deities, thereby affirming social and moral continuity from some past Golden Age. Of course, such distinctions are overdrawn, as we now know that traditional groups possess a whole range of legend, personal reminiscences and folk history that sometimes demonstrates remarkable veracity, even after millennia.[25] Yet the contrast remains illuminating and highlights the important connection between myth and material culture.

# 1

# Pottery: Forms that Endure

Once a pot has been fired, and the crystallized water is removed from the clay, it turns into a ceramic, a nearly eternal substance. It is a medium almost alone in resisting the decaying power of the jungle (stone is more resistant than earthenware but is extremely rare in this muddy, alluvial world where even pebbles become heirloom pottery polishers). Moreover, being the most plastic of all the additive crafts it unwittingly retains much information for the observant student: from a reconstruction of lost basketry techniques based on the impressions they left on a mat turntable, to the accidental corn kernel a vessel retains in its paste, thus testifying to early cultivation. The transparency of this medium means one can also divine everything, from which hand the artisan used to work with to the intricacy of his/her supernatural beliefs. Pottery, in short, makes possible a kind of ceramic sociology and ethnology.

Lowland pottery bears the paradox of all New World ceramics, being at once both very primitive and highly sophisticated. Fabricated almost exclusively by hand-building techniques like coiling (in a world where the wheel and wheel-throwing were unknown) and simple low-fire technology, it nevertheless represents some of the technically most developed and aesthetically most affecting pottery ever constructed. Millennia of experimentation have yielded the modern polychrome pottery of riverine groups like the Shipibo and the Canelos Quichua. Their thin-walled, complex silhouette pottery is made possible by the technological innovation of organic silica tempering, which anticipated the advantages of modern composites like fiberglass-

impregnated ceramics. Both ceramic complexes represent some of the most beautiful terra-cotta pottery traditions in the world today, yet are but a pale reflection of the lost glories of late prehistoric Marajoara Lower Amazon forms. The Canelos Quichua of eastern Ecuador are noted for their elegant, thin pots painted with reptilian designs and many imaginative effigies, even including representations of modern petroleum explorers and animated bracket fungus.[26] For if in the Old World pottery was a mere container, in the New it is utilitarian sculpture that happens to contain food or drink. Bowls sprout modeled heads, plates turn into recumbent armadillos, and even humble cook pots feature incised decoration.

One can even tell the ecological orientation of a group by looking at the differential complexity of its pottery. It has been demonstrated that only groups that have the political muscle to dominate long stretches of the main river can marshall all the tempers, clays, paints, resins and other resources to make such complex pottery possible.[27] Equally important, I believe, is the fact that canoe travel along the connected waterways facilitated the exchange of ideas and the play of fashion, particularly in the elaborate beer fiestas which were a periodic feature of this lifeway. The big riverine villages could support the large number of artists, craft specialists and sophisticated audiences that make elaborate ceramic art both possible and sustainable.

The mutual references between myth and material culture obtain in ceramics as in the other arts. Myths throughout the Amazon basin attest to the natural modeling parallels of the growing coils of clay. Snakes coil and

*Opposite*
**30 A Tukuna narrow-necked jar with vertical strap handles and post-fire crusting.**

**31–2 Two Shipibo-Conibo polychrome, pre-fire painted *masato* storage-fermentation jars, called *chomo ani*. These vessels are surviving examples of the most complex painted polychrome terra-cotta tradition in the South Amerindian lowlands. The larger one (bottom) is an old specimen, collected circa 1940. It has appliquéd human features on either side.**

uncoil cooperatively to form the first vessels, and even today the large porous jars housing the fermenting manioc beer of the lowlands are said to hiss with the breath of vipers as they provide their benevolent "sting" of intoxication.[28] The multi-globular stacked bodies of Shipibo pots reflect the separate origins of their "design donors," the anaconda-based designs on the lower registers and the designs derived from the Southern Cross on the upper registers. Figurines like the famous ceramic dolls of the Karajá reveal their notions of feminine pulchritude in heavy thighs and voluptuous lower bodies, while anthropomorphic Shipibo beer jars echo the Caimito archaeological burial urns upon which they were patterned. Everywhere, deliberate symbolic associations link women with pottery, from the aquatic and soft basis of the clays out of which the pots are made to the round and hollow forms of the vessels themselves. So too does the ubiquitous association of women and the serving of alcoholic beverages metonymically imitate both the rot=fermentation of the menstruation process and the seductive offer of intoxication from the hand of a solicitous woman.

The culmination of a 10,000-year experimentation with pottery was reached in the late prehistoric polychrome pottery style that spread widely, beginning about A.D. 1000, across language families and ethnic groups in the lowlands. The essence of this widespread style was the technological perfection of pre-fire polychrome slip paints derived from ochres, ores and clays to produce elaborate designs protected by a glossy post-fire resinous crusting that gives the appearance of a glazed surface. This

shiny look appealed to lowland South Amerindians who already had a bias for the light and bright in hue and chroma, as we will see from their feather art. In addition, a long process of trial and error technology brought a crowning discovery – the use of organic tempering.[29] Unlike other forms of tempering, such as ground potsherd or sand, this organic silica actually strengthens the resultant pottery once it has been fired. It makes possible extraordinary earthenware ceramic forms since the long filaments of organic silica actually act like the iron reinforcing rods in ferro-concrete, thereby giving pottery the needed resiliency to support extremely thin walls and sustain complex shapes and elaborate appendages like handles, rims and appliqué figurative adornment. Multi-globular forms, effigy vessels and carinated or pointed-shouldered vessels, such as those of the Shipibo, could now be built in sections by the traditional coiling process, thereby allowing women to specialize in various size categories and vessel shapes.

Even here the "theme and variations" logic of art holds. Most Shipibo beer jars appear to be similar, but within one of its dimensions – the shoulder region – each woman can give her pots their distinctive form. Some prefer a sharply carinated "flying saucer" shape, others squared-off shoulders, and still others shoulders of exaggerated roundness. Moreover, though all the pots look alike to a Western eye, each one must carry its own unique tissue of geometric designs. The Shipibo woman would agree with the aesthetician José Ortega y Gasset, "In art, repetition is nothing."[30]

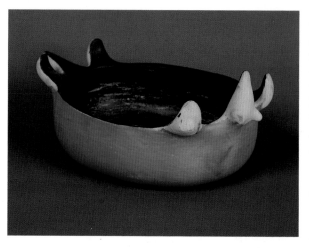

**37** Karajá ceramic figurines representing a seated man and woman. Originally, they served as dolls for Karajá girls and were modeled by their mothers. In accord with the pervasive sexual complementarity of the lowlands, these figurines are always produced in male-female pairs. The female's exaggerated thighs reveal Karajá notions of feminine pulchritude. The painting on these figurines accurately reflects the body painting worn as almost the only "clothing" by members of this tribe. It is produced from the indelible blue-black dye of the *genipa americana* fruit pod and lasts for several weeks before it wears off and must either be reapplied or replaced with different, though related, designs.

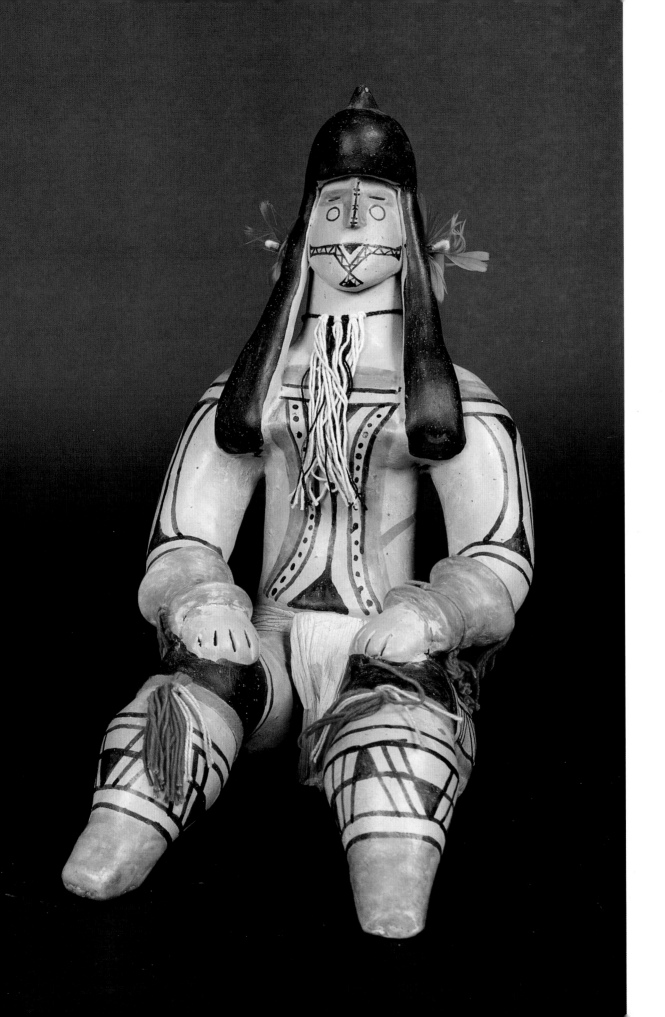

# Basketry: Inspired by the Dragon

If pots are heavy, rigid and comparatively non-portable, and therefore suited to the sedentary life along the river as lived by Canoe Indians, then lightweight and flexible basketry – containers made from rainforest llianas and fronds – is the carrying device of choice for the forest-dwelling Foot Indians. Indeed, there is often trade between the two, as when the Shipibo trade their famous pots to the interfluvial Campa for the latter's strong burden baskets, the *kantiri*. But baskets are not just containers for jungle dwellers. They are also soft, hollow receptacles that can be related analogically to the animal symbols populating lowland thought. Twill-weave plaited baskets, the hallmark of the Guianas, were once caimans that devoured people; now they "consume" possessions like the famous Waiwai telescoping men's vanity bags, which contain a man's feathers and paint as well as a shaman's crystals and other ritual paraphernalia. In this "devouring" aspect, baskets mimic reptiles which swallow their victims whole. The shimmering twill-weave construction of these same baskets recalls the glinting, textured skins of the reptiles.

Aesthetically, the most impressive lowland baskets are made from twill-weave. This is a variant of plaiting, the simplest kind of handwoven basketry, often found in the stronger wicker-weave burden baskets. In twill-weave, the "over-floating" and "under-floating" elements pass over or under more than one crossing element, producing a stepped pattern. When the surface of one of the elements is coated with a black dye, as is done in the Guianas and elsewhere in the lowlands, the result is a bichromatic basketry where one face has simple, stylized designs formed by contrasting elements. Because of

the natural form of the diagonal-crossing splints most twill-weave designs are variants on triangles, diamonds and step-motifs. I think that these "snake-like" designs mimic the coiled bodies of serpents and other long reptilian creatures like the caiman. Additionally, many of the largest and most dangerous snakes in the lowlands have diamond-like patterns, such as the mighty anaconda and the deadly fer-de-lance. In myth, then, one finds groups like the Waiwai, who derive the designs on their baskets from the skin of a slain "Dragon," the malevolent Urufiri, a monstrous creature based on anaconda and other elements. This makes the Dragon yet another of the withholding animal figures at the beginning of time who naturally possessed the skills of culture – designs – by wearing them on their bodies. Now men and women paint the Dragon's designs on their bodies as a learned, cultural act. Another of the natural donors of designs is the jaguar with its beautiful cross-like spots. Yet both of these naturally decorated creatures are dangerous cannibals, devourers of humans. Perhaps it is the "carnivorous" origin of such designs that explains why they are often considered "toxic" and why women are not permitted to use such "painted" baskets when they engage in life-crisis rites where their cultural state is most vulnerable, such as puberty rites, and must make due with monochromatic "fasting baskets."[31]

There is evidence that Yekuana flat serving baskets, made by men, are "cosmograms" of their universe, not only models of the flat hemisphere of the dome of the heavens, but also circular fields filled with complex designs representing atmospheric elements and animal symbols

*Opposite*

**38  A Tapirapé sack-shaped twill-weave seed storage basket.**

**39  A Waiwai contrast-woven, twill-weave, rectangular man's telescoping storage basket (*fakara*) with a beetle design on the upper register and a jaguar on the lower register, and feather danglers. Men store their feathers and shamans their ritual paraphernalia, such as rattles, in these "vanity bags."**

associated with various aspects of the world. In addition, baskets are associated with the respective sexes by their actual form and fabrication technology: straight, twill-weave decorated baskets are male; curved, wicker-weave plain baskets are female; and each stage of the life cycle is marked by a reciprocal exchange of baskets between the sexes.[32]

This sexual exchange evokes the second major metaphor for viewing the arts of the Amazon: gendered technology. Just as every animal comes in male and female versions, so too do the artifacts made from natural materials tend to be specialized in the complementary labor of men and women. Ironically, modern Western academics have discovered gender at precisely the point that it is becoming less relevant in the cultural context of an androgynous, power-assisted, information-driven technology that can be manipulated interchangeably by either sex. The situation in the jungle is quite the reverse; the pervasive sexual division of labor segregates every task into male and female components and then makes the contributions of the sexes complementary, so that neither sex can survive without the other. This gendered technology is not only based on the different strengths and energies of each sex (upper-body/arms/chest weapons technology for men versus lower-body/pelvic implement technology for women), but is also represented by sex-typed artifacts emblematic of each sex, which the other may not touch or utilize once they are completed. The common artifacts associated with males are weapons: bow-and-arrow, blowgun, axe, spear, war club; for women, the burden basket, baby sling, dagger and digging stick. Many field photographs of

women in the lowlands show them bent forward at a 45° angle under an enormous burden basket with a tump-line pressing against their foreheads.[33] Women's shorter stature and wider pelvises give them a more secure stance than men. Yet the meat men hunt cannot be eaten without cooking it on the fires women make from the firewood they haul from their gardens, nor can meat be eaten without the carbohydrates grown by women. And although women cultivate and harvest those cultigens and that firewood which is first cut down in slash-and-burn swiddening by men with axes, they could not exist without the prior intervention of men.

However, since skill levels and hand-eye coordination are essentially equivalent between the sexes, work in compliant media, like basketry, may sometimes be accomplished by either sex in the lowlands; in one society ceramics or basketry, while frequently associated with women, may be practiced by men – as in the Guianas among the Yekuana, where it is the men who produce the elaborate baskets for their women. Yet in "crossing over" to a feminine domestic art, the men may be the exception that proves another rule. Cross-culturally, there is a statistically significant association between women artists and geometric patterning, and men artists and representational or stylized art. This is usually attributed to the "tyranny of warp and weft" that geometricizes many designs by its very construction method, and the fact that textiles and basketry, which both exhibit this pattern, are frequently female domains. Additionally, since men are the hunters and warriors, in contact with human and non-human animals, it makes sense that their art mirrors their close visual knowledge of this "prey," for magico-religious purposes. Many of the lowland groups in which women are artists, like the Shipibo, do, in fact, produce geometric

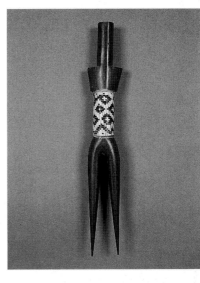

*Below:* **46 Musical instruments. Left: An Arawete split-cane rattle with feather projections. Center: A rattle-like resonator (*toque-toque*) made from a palm nut by the Pakaa Nova tribe. The rattle is the shaman's main accoutrement in curing rituals; it accompanies songs and gives emphasis to his words. Right: A giant armadillo-tail trumpet made by the Kayapó-Xikrin.**

*Bottom, left:* **47 A Waiwai cylindrical twill-weave basketry rattle with a beetle design. In recent times the seed rattling agents inside, called *shak-shak*, have been replaced by iron fragments from old Western tools or even bottle caps.**

*Bottom right:* **48 A Kayabi shallow twill-weave circular manioc flour storage basket, with a labyrinth design.**

patterning. Much of the representational art, even in new media like the crayons and paper introduced by the anthropologist, is produced by men. The test case would seem to be an art which is normally "feminine," but in some societies taken over by men. Such is the case with basketry in the Guianas – and there the basketry is filled with representational and stylized images. Thus basketry can become a major "text" in which people can encode the major animal symbols of their mythology just as easily as they can in painting or wood carving.

Basketry also illustrates the difficulty of distinguishing geometric from representational or stylized designs by the casual observer. Many of the geometric designs that structurally adorn basketry, which Western observers assume are simple decorative elements, are, in fact, representational to the people who weave them. The double fret *is* the jaguar's spots, the diamond *is* the fer-de-lance's marking, representing the animal donor they were taken from as surely as a realistic portrayal of those animals would. Geometric elements are not necessarily mere decoration.

Lastly, it is impossible to separate basketry from the other media covered in this book, such as wood-carving or feather art, since many baskets are festooned with feathers at their ends. In addition, wooden artifacts like sword clubs or daggers will have woven basketry grips, as dart quivers, rattles, or even armbands will have their bodies constructed out of twill-weave basketry. As is always the case with lowland crafts, the whole is infinitely greater and more beautiful than the parts out of which it is made.

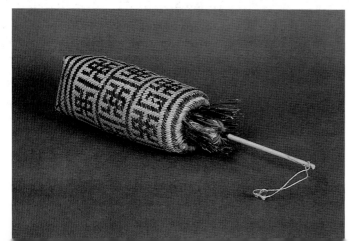

*Left:* 49 A wicker-weave burden basket with woven bands of monkey designs (*wuwa*), made by the Yekuana. The "waisted" form of this basket recalls the shape of the women who plait and use it.

*Below:* 50 A Yawalapití twill-weave, rectangular, lipped storage basket. The internal spacers temporarily hold the shape of a new basket.

*Bottom, left:* 51–2 Yekuana flat, circular twill-weave *waja* serving baskets with toad and monkey designs. Such circular baskets can be seen as microcosms of the celestial orb, with its atmospheric and animal forces. In the Guianas, for example, singing frogs herald the arrival of the rainy season; thus the vertical lines that enclose these frogs are rain symbols. Monkeys represent the upper arboreal world in the lowland cosmic hierarchy.

*Bottom, right:* 53 A Waiwai twill-weave, lipped bitter manioc flour sifter (*manari*).

# Textiles: The Spider's Loom

In most of the lowlands, textiles are comparatively underdeveloped, as in this hot and humid world the uncovered human skin is the best adaptation. The one exception is that greatest of all South Amerindian inventions, the hammock. Making them is invariably the greatest skill a woman possesses, and her most valued gift to men.[34] Hammocks are not so much woven as twined, produced on a vertical loom composed of two uprights around which their longitudinal strings are looped. The strings are then twined or knotted together by vertical strings.

Textiles assume greater importance in the ecological corridor that runs north–south along the eastern slopes of the Andes from the Oriente of Ecuador to the Yungas of Bolivia, the *montaña*. There, clothing does possess adaptive value and hence undergoes technical elaboration. In this region of high jungle, just below the cloud forest, the rainy season from December until March can be cold and windy, and clouds of mosquitoes haunt the northward-flowing rivers like the Ucayali. Woven mosquito nets make wall-less huts possible, which capitalize on the cooling power of ventilation. At the same time, the region's proximity to the Andean highlands to the west allows an interchange of textile techniques, mostly warp-patterning, to flourish. As in the highlands, a main item of dress is the poncho, basically two rectangles of hand-woven cotton cloth sewn together in the middle of the chest and on the side selvages, leaving a V-shaped opening for the head and holes for the arms. In mythology, these are human "pelts," since animals can also change their natures by taking off their "ponchos" to don the hides of other creatures or humans.

Like basketry, this technology is a feminine, lower-body material culture, deriving from the most common machine used to weave the fabric, the backstrap-loom. In this simple loom, the hard wooden parts of which are carved by men, the loom belt (usually made of deer skin won in masculine hunting) is placed around the hips of a seated woman; the other end is tied to a house post and she leans back to provide tension to the warp. Moreover, the woven product is usually worn around the hips as a wrap-around tubular skirt. Being produced from soft, cultivated tree cotton, planted and tended by women near their huts and spun with the aid of a ceramic spindle whorl of their manufacture, textiles are doubly associated with women. Congruent animal symbols, like the spider spinning her web, supply the antecedent for this feminine skill. In some lowland-derived groups like the Kogi of Colombia, the metaphor of the shuttling loom sword stands for the cyclical movements of the seasons and heavens. Modern Shipibo women have produced their own "cosmograms" in elaborately embroidered dresses using appliqué commercial bunting and Western analine-dyed yarns, as much a classic instance of the vigor of artistic hybrids (imported Western raw materials combined with Amerindian color and design sensibilities) as the intricate *repliqué* molas of the Cuna of Panama, another lowland South American-affiliated group.

A special exception to this association of women and textiles is the bark cloth of the northwest Amazon, since this is the result of a "felting" technique performed by men, who pound the soft inner bark of trees into a coarse fabric. While rough and stiff, and therefore uncomfortable as clothing, this fabric makes a perfect background for painting on frontal masks, hooded masks, wooden-mask neckpieces, crown headdress bands and utilitarian containers like dart quivers. Indeed, some of the most spectacular body dance masks made by men in lowland South America are fabricated out of painted cones of bark cloth that completely hide the body of the masquerder.

Under the rubric of textiles we can also treat beadwork, since in the *montaña* diagonal beadwork is woven using a special miniaturized backstrap-loom. Beads are also associated with women, as their round form contrasts with the sharp and pointed decorative forms of men, like spiky bird plumes or pointed canines and claws. Indeed, in Waiwai mythology the first beads were the quickly rotting round eggs of fish, the gift of the first fish woman's Anaconda People kinspeople.[35] In those cultures where men are allocated the wearing of decorative imported glass beadwork, as among the Shipibo, it is still the women who must weave these adornments for them. Beadwork, like most of these arts, rarely appears alone, but is festooned with feather finials or is wrapped around cane crowns.

Ucayali looms, the simplest of all fixed looms, characterize the interior Foot Indians like the Mayoruna of Peru, and are used to weave natural jute-like materials (rather than cotton) mostly to create that other quintessential female accoutrement, the narrow baby-carrying sling worn diagonally across the body. Significantly, this artifact conforms to the imperative of all lowland crafts that they have a design on them to be properly finished; there is no such thing as a plain baby carrier, its wefts invariably form a

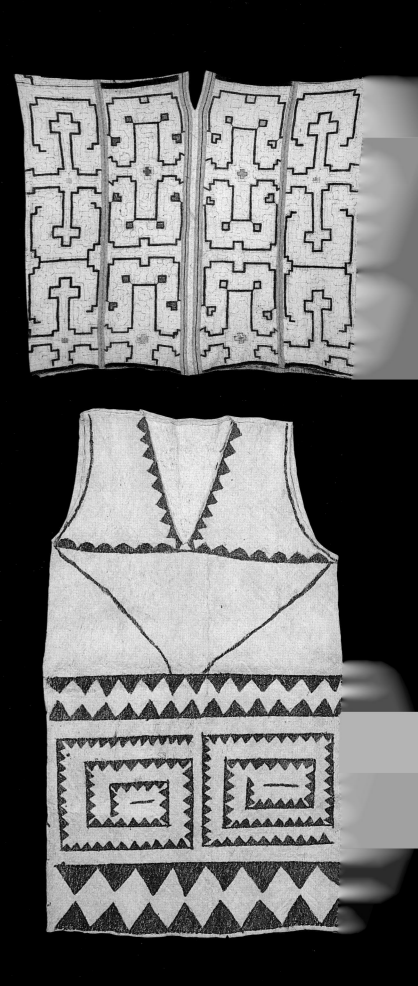

diamond pattern reminiscent of the viper's diamonds.

In the Guianas, this same framework is used to fabricate the famous split-seed women's aprons, now also made out of imported glass beads with a vertical, rather than a diagonal, beading technique. The same sequence has occurred in the *montaña* where the monochromatic beads – actually seeds – have given way to imported beads in brilliant colors.

This is another instance of the vigor of cultural hybrids. One positive byproduct of the clash of cultures resulting from European contact with the New World was Amerindian access to imported Western raw materials. The conjunction of indigenous design traditions and sophisticated color sense with Western raw materials has produced some of the most spectacular of all Amerindian accoutrements – everything from the beaded leather costumes of the North-American Great Plains Indians to the elaborate figurative molas of the Cuna of Panama. Indeed, paradoxically, our stereotype of the Native American in elaborate and colorful regalia would not have been possible without these imported materials.

The intricate costumes of the Shipibo, rivaling in elaboration those of the Cuna, are a case in point. Nineteenth-century photographs reveal dull-garbed riverine

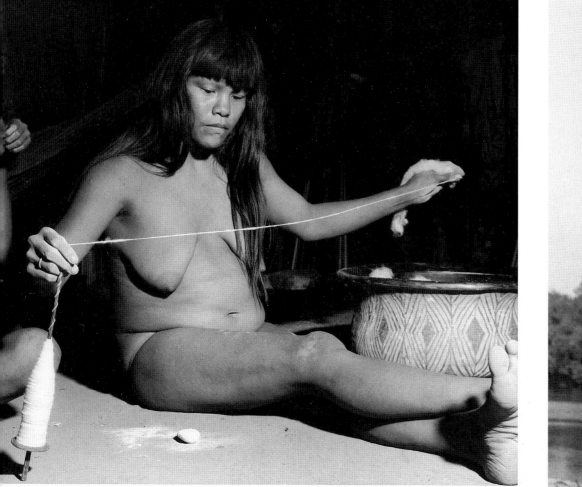

Panoans with their monochromatic black ponchos and simple seed necklaces and bandoliers, before the rubber boom of 1880–1920 gave them access to Western metals and trade beads. Contrast that somber traditional picture with the modern Shipibo man, adorned with colorful beaded chokers, bracelets and breastplates dangling with perforated antique silver Peruvian coins and dressed in a white poncho painted with intricate black designs and decorated with a central warp-patterned woven panel in bright analine dyes. The more traditional Shipibo woman embodies even more imported components, including her midriff-baring patchwork blouse made from artfully combined, patterned trade cloth, a massive belt of white imported glass beads, a carved aluminum labret in her lower lip with a central panel of cut red plastic, a nose-dangler made from a coin, and a wrap-around skirt made of *tela tropical* (machine-made plain weave patterned to look like indigenous homespun cotton) embroidered with bright analine-dyed store-bought yarn. How "native" and "conservative" she appears, how modern and innovating she really is! The "ethnic badge" of aboriginal heritage is dependent on Western technology, but the total Amerindian ensemble transcends those materials to produce a more striking effect than anything found in the donor culture.

**56** A Waurá woman spinning cotton. She is seated on the ground, the typical position for women at work in the Amazon. She wears the traditional coiffure – bangs and loose, long hair – and is naked except for a plain cord belt. The painted Waurá pot beside her holds the tree cotton out of which she is spinning her string. She uses a hafted ceramic spindle whorl of her own manufacture which she twirls with her right hand while her left teases the fibers from the cotton bolls she has removed from around their seeds. (The Waurá are the only pottery makers of the Xingú region, and trade their ware widely to other village tribes.)

**57** Jurúna women pounding manioc flour in hollowed-out cylindrical wooden mortars. They wear typical, simple, wrap-around cylindrical cotton skirts and are naked above the waist.

39

**Opposite**

61 A conical Tukuna painted bark-cloth mask.

62 A Jívaro painted bark-cloth tunic with a pectoral and a back ornament made of a toucan head, wings and pelt. The polychrome designs on this spectacular garment are rich in hallucinogenic imagery. The addition of a whole bird head and pelt asserts men's identification with the celestial birds, whose feathers also serve as danglers from the tunic's fringe. The Jívaro often use whole bird pelts on their artifacts, either stuffed as danglers or splayed as pectorals, and their favorite source of feathers is the toucan.

*Top:* 58 A glass bead apron with feather danglers made by a Wayana-Aparai woman. Compared to ill. 59, this intricate glass beaded apron shows what happens to traditional designs once Western trade goods become available, in this case colorful glass beads of Czech or Italian manufacture. These women artists have applied the rectilinear patterns on their men's twill-weave baskets to their aprons. They are, however, only allowed to use the shorter breast feathers of "celestial birds," while men regularly use their long plumes to decorate their own costumes.

*Above:* 59 A seed bead apron worn by Waiamiri-Atroari women. They cover the loins, leaving the buttocks bare. Their plain round beads echo the typically spherical forms of women's artifacts.

*Right:* 60 An Urubú-Kaapor woven cotton baby carrier used during the name-giving ceremony, the Ta'lhupi raha.

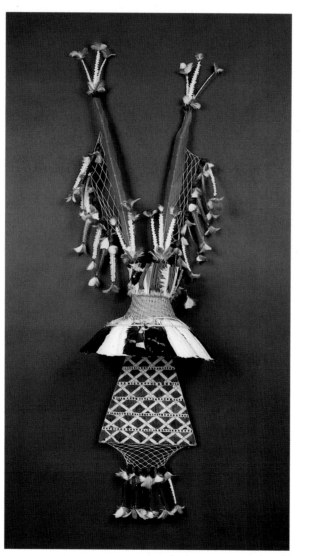

*Above:* 63 Man's cotton-string and glass-bead (upper) armbands, from the Kayapó-Kreen Akrore tribe.

*Right:* 64 A feather cap headdress of the Palikur tribe, with two feather projections and a wooden nape painted with a net design. The construction of this headdress is extremely intricate, with its openwork danglers attached by balls of wax and composite plumes. The short feathers cemented to the tips of longer ones act as weighted danglers to hurry the bobbing plumes into movement when the wearer of this headdress dances.

*Far right:* 65 A man's neck-nape back ornament with a hanging feather-and-shell trailer, from the Rikbaktsá tribe. All of the shells are carved into the shape of fish.

66 The bold, white lines highlighting the features of this fearsome circular Tukuna bark-cloth mask replicate the face paint humans apply. But here it decorates the visage of Yurupary, a hairy Forest Ogre known throughout the northwest Amazon. He is associated with hunting magic and is distantly related to the hairy Urufiri dragon of the Guianas.

67  This oval Tukuna bark-cloth Yurupary mask has real
caiman teeth. The disheveled palm-leaf raffia hair, wild,
staring eyes, and coarse-textured bark-cloth face of this
spirit evoke the forest that is its home as well as the
source of this mask's raw material.

**68** A painted wooden dance-costume mask with a bark-cloth mantle, worn by the Piaroa-Huarime tribe. Though the crude white painting on this mask looks inept when the mask is still, it effectively animates it when the dancer is in motion, reminding us of the kinetic nature of lowland arts.

*Opposite:* **69** This Tukuna carved wooden mask is attached to a painted bark-cloth body dance costume used in initiation ceremonies. The huge, incongruous ears – or perhaps large ear discs – of this helmet mask bely its serious purpose of evoking the keen hearing of the wind ghost spirits.

# Hard Carvings: A Question of Gender

**4**

Any work in obdurate materials like wood, bone or stone is commonly a masculine task in the lowlands of South America. Such gendered division of labor is extremely ancient and dates back to Pre-Columbian times when, except for in regions like the *montaña* of Peru, metals were unknown in the jungle. Instead, not terribly effective natural tools produced from the bone and shell of animals and fish had to be used to work hard tropical woods or resistant bone. Those tasks were laborious in the extreme, perhaps explaining the less-developed wood-carving in tropical America compared with tropical Africa and Asia where metal tools were used quite early. This difficulty may also explain why most lowland wood-carving is not truly three-dimensional but consists mostly of painting, incision and bas-relief on flat or columnar tree-trunk-like artifacts. Preservation does not favor the pre-contact wooden and bone artifacts in the lowlands, but under better conditions, as in the caves of the Antilles, true marvels of intricacy and craftsmanship illustrate how far skill and patience could offset rudimentary tools.

Even so, the effort required to effectively guide the dull cutting implements demanded, and still demands, much upper-body strength for precise execution, and is therefore a male preserve. Yet, this does not mean that women's contribution to wood and bone carving is negligible. Indeed, it is often essential, as among the Shipibo, who execute large and fearsome war clubs from the hard, black cortical wood of the *chonta* palm. Their experience is a common one in the lowlands that is characterized by the way in which both male and female labor is essential for even basically masculine or

feminine items of technology. Not only do given artifacts require a complementarity of sexual input, but the assigned tasks of men and women also frequently *alternate* in the same artifact. Thus, the Shipibo man's war club is a tall and formidable bladed weapon, larger than the similar Guianan war clubs. It is a masculine symbol *par excellence*, which is used for ritual wrestling and stereotyped battles between visitors from potentially friendly villages. These "sword clubs" have a wrapped basketry-sheathed pommel for a good grip, and a triangular elongated blade with a terminal notch for pinning an adversary's neck to the ground while the crown of his head is slashed to the bone with a special "scratching knife," often in reprisal for adultery. When swung with the flat of the blade such a heavy weapon could incapacitate a man by knocking his wind out, but when the weapon was swiveled in the hands and the sharp of the blade was directed at the victim, the weapon turned lethal, easily splitting a man's head like a melon. Even today, long after such battles have been outlawed by the Peruvian state, men dance with the weapon placed over their right shoulder, and also drink manioc beer after the festival, seated, but with war club still ready. Men carve miniature clubs for their sons, perfect in every detail. The war club, like all weapons designed to take a human life, must be elaborately decorated, and hence be a work of art. Each side of the blade bears its own unique incised designs, the incisions highlighted by white kaolin against an organic dye-stained black background. No woman may touch a man's war club once it has been carved, yet a woman's input is essential to finish the weapon. After carving its form, down to the

*Opposite*

*Top:* **70** A carved and painted wooden bird-effigy food-scraping spatula from the Kamayurá tribe, Xingú region. It represents a stork, or a similar long-beaked wading bird. The "stirring" action of such a bird's beak as it searches the shallows for fish and amphibians may have suggested the function of this artifact.

**71–2** Two Kayamurá carved and painted wooden bull-roarers, each having unique designs. The otherworldly whirring of these traditional artifacts heralds the arrival of the supernaturals and sends the women scurrying inside their residential huts when men hold dances in the cleared plaza. Normally made and stored in the central men's hut, forbidden to feminine intrusion, these thin objects must be painted with the traditional designs before they can be used.

elaborately shaped pommel, a man must find some woman who is related to him – a wife, a mother, a daughter – to draw the designs on the club with plant juice since women are the graphic artists in Shipibo society. I have even seen mighty warriors, who were feuding with their wives at the time, reduced to walking about the matrilocal compound forlornly looking for some woman willing to draw the designs which he then incises into the blade. The masculine weapon symbolic of phallic aggression must, in short, be decorated by a woman. It is "realized" by a man and once finished it is thereafter tabooed to her.

Other artifacts as closely associated with women as the sword club is to men must also await their male input to function, even though, once finished, no man would touch them. For example, the elaborately and elegantly carved loom swords, battens and loom bars of Shipibo backstrap-looms, quintessential technology for women as the society's weavers, must be carved by men. Thus a woman will stop weaving if she cannot get a related man to replace broken loom parts.

Some carved wooden artifacts illustrate the opposite side of the dialogue of the sexes. If the alternation of sexual production illustrates the complementarity of men's and women's tasks, then certain ritual and ceremonial artifacts reveal the intimidation and sexual antagonism that keep male and female spheres segregated. Thus while scenes of daily life throughout lowland South America depict men and women sharing a tranquil domestic life, religion paradoxically expresses the fragility of male power over females through the application of direct or indirect violence against women. Masked

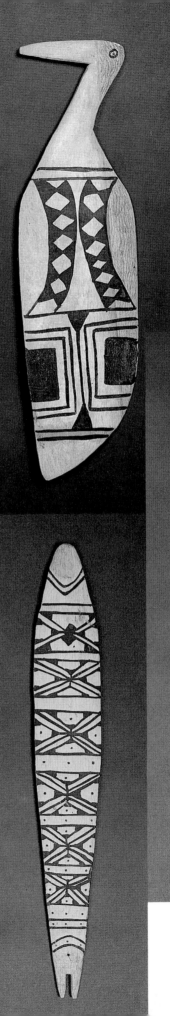

rituals are used to intimidate women,[36] who are forbidden to enter central men's huts on penalty of gang rape, and are regularly assaulted with over-sized phallic images in ceremonies. Or, in other regions, both sexes line up in the village plaza and hurl insults at each other, women "ejaculating" kernels of corn while making derogatory remarks about the men's sexual equipment, while men shoot arrows between the legs of their assailants and refer to myths of emasculating women. These bizarre performances acquire the force of logic through myth. In Beginning Time, the phallus was held by the women, and used to subjugate men, and in current mythic space women still retain the aggressive upper hand, as in the widespread belief in a tribe of nomadic and warlike Amazons who abduct, rape and kill men to reproduce themselves. Such dangerous imagined women are conceptually subjugated in masculine thought by being defined as artifacts actually constructed by men (as the first woman was a Wooden Bride carved by a masculine figure out of a tree), so becoming a part of culture only by men's activity. Thus men can retain their rule over women by denying women's role in culture (the real facts to the contrary notwithstanding) and treating them as animals, easily led astray by aquatic or sylvan animal seducers out of culture and back into nature whence they came.

On a mythic level this also leads to womb envy and the masculine appropriation of reproduction where hollow gourds or even the hollow skulls of the trophy head cult, carved or adorned by men, become the portable wombs in which men mythically and/or symbolically conceive children (thereby demoting women's contribution to gestation to that of a passive container). It has been shown how the sex so avidly engaged in is also an anxious pleasure, filled with potentially dangerous effects on men, devoured by women in sex.[37]

**73 Two wooden dolls representing "were-creatures," made by the Piaroa-Huarime tribe.**

I have related this paradox of sexual attraction/antagonism as a way of dealing psychologically with the rigid construction of the opposite sex in the pervasive sexual division of labor that characterizes the lowlands. If in every task one depends on the contribution of the opposite sex, it is easy to feel that the other gender is getting the better of a bad deal. This leads to anger and resentment, but rather than expressing it as individual husbands beating wives (though that also occurs), lowland South Amerindians' convention of masking feelings requires that the antagonism be expressed publicly and generically against *all* men or *all* women, so that it can be healed through the public catharsis of ceremony.

Accordingly, the largest and most impressive carved wooden artifacts such as the giant, flat, hemispherical Tapirapé enemy warrior masks, the *upé*, or *ypé* (ills. 83–4), also comment upon the segregation, yet complementarity, of men and women. Collectively called *tawa*, these huge half-moon shaped masks are the most complex artifact the Tapirapé make and represent their Kayapó and Karajá enemy warriors killed in battle. They may also evoke history by symbolizing the human trophy heads kept by their ancient warlike Tupinambá ancestors along the distant Brazilian coast. The soul of the dead warrior becomes an *anchunga* (a spirit) and is appropriated by the Tapirapé to grant hunting success, since the emergence of these masked figures is the most important herald of the dry season, the major hunting epoch. As they represent the masculine potency of war, the masks are carved in secret in the men's hut by members of the Bird Societies, dual organizations, or moieties, internally divided into age groups, that organize songfests (modeled on the protocultural songs of birds) and collective hunts. Freshwater pearls provide the flashing eyes of the figures, colored in a quadrant system by a resin-adhered feather mosaic of red, yellow and blue macaw breast and tail feathers and carrying a crown of fringing feathers (which at an earlier time were anchored by long black hawk feathers evoking the fierce qualities of this raptor). The feather nimbus, which artfully fits into a wrapped-splint channel around the mask's periphery so that it can be "unzipped" and stored separately between performances, ends in fiery red macaw tail feathers. Holes into the soft wood of the mask's body are made by burning, and beeswax provides the black gums into which the peg canines are fastened for a gaping mouth. Completing the face, the freshwater mother-of-pearl feathered circlets below the eyes are actually the head's ear plugs shifted by an artistic convention.

Impressive as it is, the mask itself is but one element of the full dance costume worn by the men when they emerge from the men's hut to dance in the plaza. They are covered in a skirt, a cape and a headdress of *burití* palm fiber which hides their identity, except for their exposed hands and feet, from the surrounding women who are meant to regard them as the spirits incarnate. However, many women do recognize specific men by their voices and feet, but cannot declare this knowledge aloud. As the costume is more than the mask, so too is the performance more than the ensemble of male dancers, who usually dance in pairs to symbolize the moieties of the Bird Societies. Their women form an essential peripheral audience whose job it is to witness the dance and offer drink to the shuffling spirits.[38] In similar masked Kuikúru ceremonies the carved bull-roarer, decorated with complex geometric arrays (ill. 74),[39] becomes the voice of the spirits who announce the arrival of such masculine symbols of power in the cleared plaza. Its whirring roar intimidates the women and keeps them shut up in their fringing residences while the men dance.

Not all artifacts carved by men express sexual conflict, however. Some embody the positive aspects of the nurturing male. Thus, besides the carved war club and the wooden or gourd mask, the low men's stool is his most powerful and enduring accoutrement. Frequently carved in the image of a standing predator on which men model themselves, like a jaguar or a caiman, these stools are the ultimate power object of both the shaman and the warleader/headman/chief. The creator-culture heroes assumed the shamanic stance, head in hands, elbows on knees, and thought the world into being while seated on their stools. Other stools, carved to represent two-headed birds, are the vehicles that allow the shaman to fly through the levels of the universe. Archaeological figurines, often modeled out of enduring ceramics, depict high-status men seated erect on their stools. Polished black wooden stools and cult figures, encrusted with white shell or gleaming gold plaques, expressed hierarchy throughout the Guianas and the Antilles, and were widely traded. The sexual component is also present in this hierarchy of carved wood: men sit above the ground on hard stools they have carved while women sit on soft woven mats on the ground *below* them, just as men sling their hammocks above women.

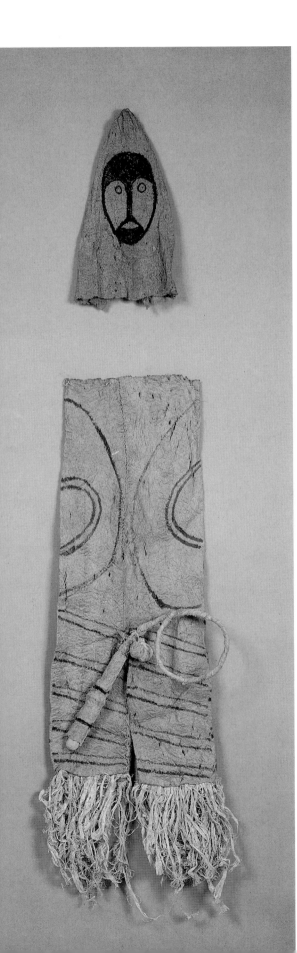

Stools, carved out of a single piece of wood, are the indispensable male accoutrement in the lowlands. These represent the male shaman's or headman's "power objects."

*Above:* 77 A Yekuana-tribe openwork, triangular-footed, feline effigy stool. Feline effigies represent strength and ferocity. When seated on this feline, men acquire such power. The small head, long neck and absence of spots may identify this feline as the retiring "deer jaguar," the cougar or mountain lion. Similar stools have been identified in the literature as jaguar effigies.

*Right:* 78 A column-footed painted jaguar effigy stool, Jurúna tribe.

*Below:* 79 A double-headed monkey effigy stool, carved and painted, with tabular feet and feather danglers, Karajá tribe.

*Above:* 80 A two-headed (inverted "T"-shape) footed bird effigy stool, Kalapálo tribe. The painted water motifs suggest that it represents a mythical aquatic bird. The double-headed aspect of this stool (and ill. 79) underscores the pervasive dualism of lowland art and thought.

81 A footed bird effigy stool made by the Kamayurá. The feet have an inverted "T"-shape. Bird effigies function as the winged vehicles on which men fly to the Sky World to commune with the celestial spirits, chiefly the Sun; they are, in effect, the shaman's "airplanes."

82  Three round, wax-modeled,
animal-effigy dance masks
painted with white clay, made
by the Piaroa-Huarime. The wax
and clay cover a fiber frame
that has been coated by bark
cloth. They have fiber mantles.
Left and center:  These dance
masks represent marmosets,
small New-World prosimians
who are usually assimilated to
monkeys in lowland thought,
often with some affinity to
humans. Right:  This dance
mask represents a vampire bat.
Because of their carnivorous
nature and sinister quality of
attack, vampires are equated
with Forest Ogres in lowland
thought, and as denizens of the
night, bats generally stand for
the Dawn World of Beginning
Time.

83  A Tapirapé *upé* ("enemy warrior") mask. These semi-circular wooden masks are the largest and most distinctive produced in the lowlands. Constructed of blue, yellow and scarlet macaw feathers affixed to a wooden panel with beeswax, they have a splint border into which a feather fringe, the spirit's headdress, is inserted. Traditional masks, such as ill. 84 (opposite), have a central cross of red feathers. This mask, however, has a cross of blue and yellow feathers, which is derived from the similar coloring of the Brazilian flag. The fringing feather diadem "unzips" for separate storage, the flashing rectangular eyes are freshwater mother-of-pearl inserts, and the pearl roundels on the cheeks are actually meant to represent the figure's ear plugs, moved inward on the face by artistic convention.

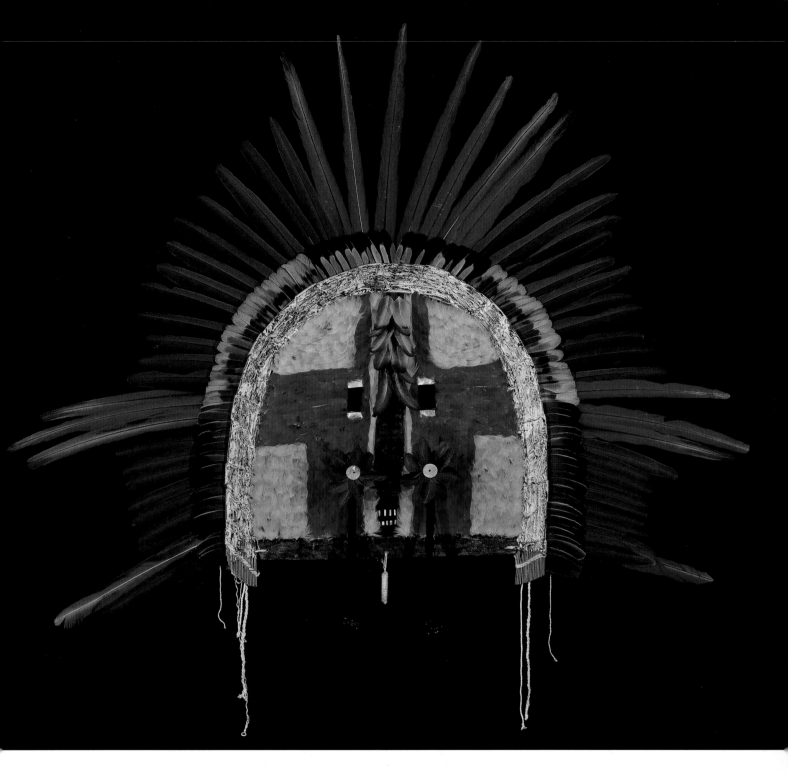

**84** A Tapirapé *upé* trophy-head mask commemorating someone of importance who has died. The presence of a double row of feathers further distinguishes this *upé* mask from the one opposite. Also called *cara grande* ("big face") in local Portuguese, they are carved in the central men's hut, the *takana*. Originally, they represented the trophy heads of defeated enemy warriors, but in the present pacified times, they are said to represent the spirits of those Tapirapé who have died in the past year.

# Featherwork: Gift of the Birds

The other ultimate power object of men, besides the war club, mask and stool, is made of softer, but still gleaming material – the condensed fire of the feather headdress. Here the same sexual cross-fertilization of objects takes place as with wood-carving; while men make of themselves something cultural, distinguishing themselves in the process from the animals of nature, they must do so by appropriating the raw materials of nature itself, and replicating in their activities the principles of natural life. Like peacocks, men in South Amerindian society are the strutting, decorated dandies, not women. Their upper bodies sprout plumes and animal teeth, while the lower bodies (loins) of women display more modest and sparse decoration like natural seed-bead aprons or a simple string hip belt. A central panoply of festooned male dancers replicates the mating grounds of tropical forest birds like the golden cock-of-the-rock. In a cleared area during an orgy of sexual selection, men, like birds, put on a display for drab, but choosy, females. In doing so, they not only identify with celestial birds, but also wear their plumes.

In accord with the pervasive dualism of Amerindian thought, there are not just birds or bird plumes, as Western nomenclature would have it, but masculine and feminine birds. Thus the analyst must carefully note which bird feather goes where, from what species it derives and how it is colored or patterned. He/she must consult the ornithological literature to register various birds' range, behavior and morphology, and even then will not know as much as the people who studied, hunted, observed and ultimately appropriated the feathers. Plumes are used for color, as mosaics or as unitary objects, spikes of hue and chroma. Unlike Westerners who regarded gold as the ultimate wealth, the lowlanders and the highland and coastal peoples with whom they traded plumes and captive birds saw feathers as the most valued goods. The color energies of the feathers, evanescent and soon devoured by insect pests, no matter how carefully stored, call up in sympathetic magical manner the natural forces they emulate. According to Waiwai shamans, when the Sun refuses to shine he puts on his black-feathered curassow headdress, as evidenced by the dark, rain-swollen clouds above their Guianan highland home. Hence, to call out the Sun, one must don a white-hot harpy eagle or great egret headdress (like ill. 119), or a burning bright scarlet macaw headdress, in the hopes that the Sun will emulate the shaman's changing of crowns. Color is everywhere.

The reciprocity between myths and artifacts establishes that every artifact can be read as a text just as every text (recorded oration) comments on an object. Moreover, each text is itself a complex compound of components. For example, in cultures where hair carries more than its usual freight of libidinal symbolism, the Waiwai hair-tube, into which adult men insert their single long pigtail, ends in a bulb of feathers from various species that recapitulate the levels of the rainforest from which their "bird-donors" were taken. Thus at the forest-floor level are dull, dark-plumaged birds, reluctant fliers all, such as the turkey-like curassow – feminine birds, identified with these lower realms. The curassow was the bird "instructor" of the first people, and told them how to thatch their huts. The communal hut is both the symbol and the actual site of genealogical continuity; one village, one hut, one people. Hence, curassow feathers form the lowest mass of the feather bulb that hangs low on the back of a man's body, level with his buttocks.

In the layered world that is the rainforest, the next level up is the middle canopy within which the brightly colored, fast-flying "celestial birds" wing their way in search of fruits and nuts. These raucous birds are the toucans and scarlet macaws. Hence, above the black curassow feathers are found the bright red, orange and yellow fringe of toucan breast feathers encircling the middle of the feather bulb on a Waiwai man's hair-tube terminus.[40] The long tail feathers of the scarlet macaw sprout upward from men's upper-arm ligatures or dangle from them, giving them wings with which to fly across the plaza in dance. All over the lowlands men are birds and direct their gaze upward to the Sky World above their Earth World, where the bird spirits dwell, acting as messengers of the benevolent Sun.

Lastly, in the upper canopy at the very top of giant *ceiba* trees, world-tree armatures of the multi-layered worlds, lie the bone-strewn nests of those awesome high fliers, the giant harpy eagles. Among the largest eagles in the world, they are the raptor hunters of New World monkeys like thirty-pound howlers and smaller capuchins. Men emulate them as hunters and warriors, capture them and place them in special huts, actually cages in the middle of the masculine plaza, there to use the large raptors as living donors of their filmy down feathers and whitish-gray crest plumes. Nevertheless, harpies are denigrated in myth as cannibal ogres for precisely the same reasons that they are emulated in

sartorial art: secret admiration. Harpy feathers thus decorate the uppermost fringe of the hair-tube feather bulb, and eagle down is pasted to the oil-slicked hair of dancers, to fly from their heads in a white snowlike flurry in the active passion of dances. The erect plumes from the eagle's head give male warriors a crest of their own in the form of the feather headdresses. Therefore, each vertical zone of the human body, the micro-cosmos, corresponds to the appropriate level of the multiple nested worlds of the forest itself. These zones are recapitulated not only in the zones of the body, but also in the communal hut within which this decorated body dwells. The round house's soft, low-growing palm thatch, harvested by women, forms the lowest shingles; higher up the cone is a stiffer, taller-growing palm thatch harvested by men. The conical roof ends in a tall, protruding, phallic center post (not structurally necessary for the hut, but brought in through the single vaginal door in an act of symbolic intercourse), which ends in a single, round, feminine, gourd finial. People thus live within a self-copulating organism; the hut lives and breathes with the exhalations of its sleeping "children" as the hammocks softly rock with nocturnal nuptial couplings.

The macro-cosmos does not stop with the hut and the village, but spreads outward on the flat, circular Earth World on which humans dwell in a series of concentric rings of alternating, sexually identified activity zones. (From center to periphery the rings of this gendered space are: [1] the masculine central house post and/or central men's hut, [2] peripheral feminine sleeping areas and/or fringing family huts, [3] the central cleared male dance plaza, [4] the encircling female-affiliated trash-yards, bathing places and secondary forest with house gardens, [5] the masculine-aligned deep forest periphery.) Feather art, made from forest birds but

destined for central cultural use by men, travels inward from the sacred periphery, to reside in the sacred center (as caged bird donors or sequestered feather headdresses), and then moves outward again into the dance plaza in a flight of life and light.

If the feathered macro-cosmos has a horizontal dimension, like the encircling plumed ligatures and belts of the human body, then it also has a vertical aspect comparable to the ankles-waist-neck-and-head zones of the standing befeathered person. It begins in the middle, with the hut and its central house post as the *axis mundi*; below it is a subaquatic Underworld, affiliated with feminine principles and reptilian life forms, and above it arches a masculine Sky World of avian and solar spirits.[41] The feathered headdress and the wings of plumes that rise from the upper arm ligatures of men thus transform them into birds who have swooped down from the Sky World to visit the world of humans, bringing with them the gifts of culture stolen from the stingy beings below. Feathers truly are fragments of the sky.

*Right:* 87 A panoramic picture of a Kamayurá village (Upper Xingú, eastern Brazil) showing, from left to right, the flute house where the sacred *jakui* flutes are stored, the harpy-eagle cage in the center of the plaza, and an oval communal hut, the *maloca.*

*Opposite:* 88 Inside its cage hut, a harpy eagle spreads its powerful wings, waiting to be the reluctant donor of its plumes for headdresses like the Waurá crown (ill. 99). The eagle is not killed; its feathers are collected when it molts. In the meantime, the giant raptor serves as an impressive symbol of the village.

*Below:* 89 Yanomamö men's armbands of curassow head-pelts with white heron and scarlet macaw feather projections and feather danglers. Often worn in sets of two, these above-bicepts ligatures give men "wings" in emulation of the bird spirits.

*Right:* 90 A Karajá feather mosaic cap headdress with a scarlet macaw plume projection, usually worn during the initiation ceremonies.

*Opposite:* 91 An upper-arm, radial feather projection "wing" ensemble from the Mashco Amarakaeri tribe, Peruvian *montaña*. This intricate ensemble (which includes macaw plumes, parrot feathers, fiber, monkey teeth, snail shells and bird pelts) gives an accurate impression of the complexity of lowland sartorial decorations. Worn during initiation, it declares that the initiate is eligible for marriage.

*Left:* 92 A Kayapó-Xikrin man's freshwater mother-of-pearl necklace with glass beads and cotton fiber strands (*ngapokredje*). Children may wear this necklace on a daily basis but adult men only on ceremonial occasions.

*Below:* 93 A man's harpy-eagle bone and scarlet macaw plume necklace (*awa-tukaniwar*) with neck bands composed of regularly overlapping hummingbird breast feathers. Made by the Urubú-Kaapor, it is worn during the name-giving ceremony.

*Bottom, left:* 94 Urubú-Kaapor dangling earrings, illustrating the use of feathers for color, as well as the canny exploitation of tiny breast feathers on iridescent hummingbirds in lowland arts.

*Opposite:* 95 An Urubú-Kaapor woman's necklace (*tukaniwar*), the feminine counterpart of ill. 93, with a centerpiece composed of iridescent blue hummingbird breast and black wing feathers.

*Below:* 96, 98 Men's feathered headbands made by the Jívaro. The ring crown (top) clearly illustrates the cane framework that underlies most lowland headdresses.

*Right:* 97 Jívaro cane headbands showing the modular construction of many lowland headdresses. Top: A toucan breast-feather pelt headband with a central diadem of parrot feathers and a scarlet macaw plume. Here, a central diadem and projecting feathers are added to a simple bird breast pelt ring headdress. Ironically, this can be worn by a woman if her husband has first earned the right to wear the more common, simpler ring form (bottom). Traditionally, men were only entitled to wear the simpler headdresses after they had killed a man.

*Opposite:* 99 A Waurá man's feather crown headdress with feather projections and a central diadem (*tukanape*). This elaborate headdress adds projecting harpy eagle feathers and a central scarlet macaw diadem to the more common Xinguano form. It is worn during dance ceremonies such as the Javari and the Kuarup.

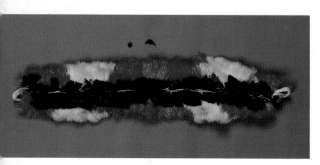

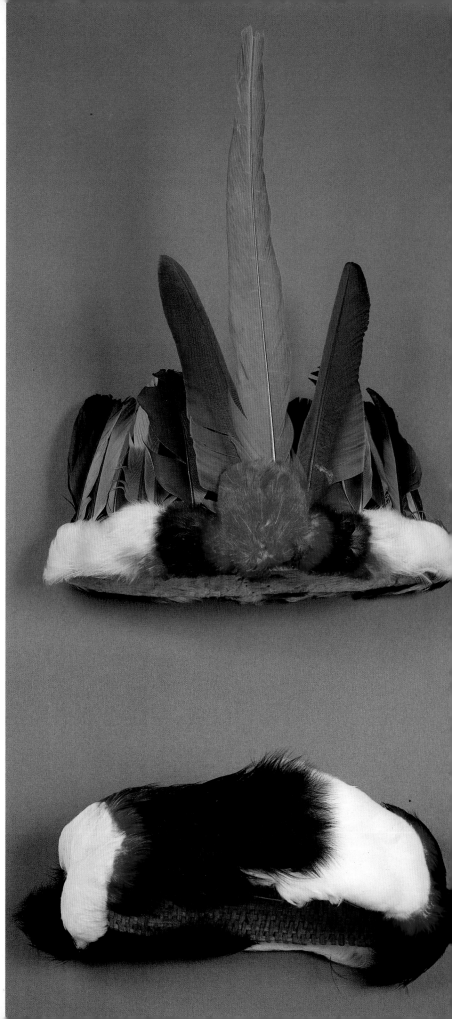

**100** A Rikbaktsá man's radial feather headdress with feather danglers. The lower feather danglers imitate the tail of the bird, the body being the feather circlet.

*Opposite:* **101** A man's radial feather headband headdress with a nape (*myhara*), made by the Rikbaktsá. It may be inspired by the famous 19th-century *mundurucú* feather cap headdress with a nape.

charismatic individuals destined to become great *pajés*, or shamans, withstand Thunder's assault and are able to finish the dance with the headdress still firmly on their heads.

**104** A Tapirapé Topu wax figurine with an elongated neck. As the agents of Thunder, these small supernaturals, swooping low in miniature celestial canoes, fill aspiring shamans with their little arrows, thereby sending them into a catatonic trance until a strong candidate resists their powers. Thunder is an angry being who dwells in his black cumulo-nimbus cloud-home, shooting gigantic lightning-bolt arrows at the people the shamans seek to protect.

*From left to right*

**102** The Kaó singing ceremony cap headdress with a radial macaw-feather projection, made by the Tapirapé. The red band above the white down feathers that compose the cap consists, in fact, of elaborate rosettes made out of macaw breast feathers. These headdresses are worn by pairs of noted singers from the Bird Societies and herald the collective hunts the societies organize at the end of the rainy season.

**103** A man's radial headdress, with a trussed bamboo headband frame projecting behind. This headdress plays a role in the most dramatic (Kawió) ceremony in Tapirapé culture, in which successive aspirants to the role of shaman put the headdress on their heads only to fall into a rigid trance, shot down by the arrows of the Topu (see ill. 104), the irascible dwarf familiars of Thunder, the most prominent supernatural. Dark Thunder, of course, is enraged by the burning scarlet macaw plumes that symbolize his nemesis, the Sun. Eventually,

*Left:* 105, 107 Frontal (top) and dorsal view of an *akangatar*, a man's radial macaw-feather headdress with cotton danglers. It is worn during the Urubú-Kaapor name-giving ceremonies.

*Above:* 106 This *akangatar* uses yellow *oropendola* feathers.

*Opposite*
108–11 Radial headdresses. Left to right, top to bottom: a man's "nimbus" *pariko* made by the Bororo and worn only during the festival of the dead; a Kayabi egret-feather headdress with a central diadem of scarlet macaw plumes; an *ompolok*, an *oropendola* feather headdress, made by the Txikao (the black inner circlet consists of wrapped cane splints); and a Kayabi *oropendola* feather headdress.

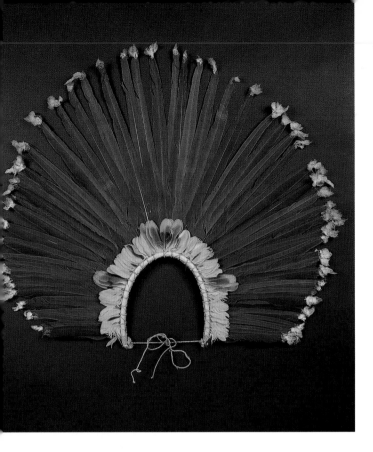

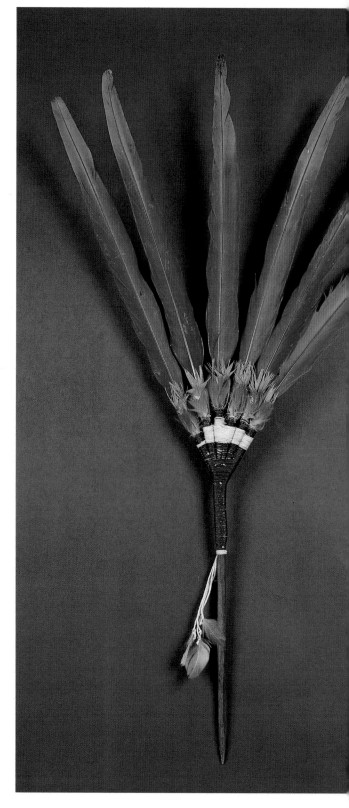

**112** A Kayapó-Mekranoti feather cap headdress with a central plume projection of yellow *oropendola* feathers. The lower feathers are from the blue and yellow macaw. These caps are related to the Karajá *lori-lori* cap headdresses.

**113** A Kayapó-Mekranoti feather hair pin worn on the back of the head. Its primary feathers are from the scarlet macaw.

*Opposite:* **114** A Kayapó-Mekranoti *roriro*, a feather cap headdress with a scarlet macaw plume as a central projection. The lower band on the headdress is composed of black curassow feathers.

**115–17 Three Kayapó-Txukahamae headdresses.**
*Above:* A feather cap headdress with feather danglers and a central feather projection. *Top, right:* A cane crown with scarlet macaw plume projections and a central diadem (*okoiaki*). *Right:* A scarlet macaw plume headdress with a cane-and-cotton support roundel (*krokroti*) worn on the back of the head. The radial plumes end in white egret down feather finials.

*Opposite:* 118 A Kayapó-Xikrin man's cylindrical cane crown (*krua-pu*) with *oropendola* feather projections and central front and rear macaw plume diadems.

**119** A cylindrical cane crown headdress with filmy white egret feather projections and scarlet macaw plumes, made by the Waiwai. A variant of this headdress utilizes harpy-eagle breast-feathers instead of egret plumes. The Waiwai consider this to be the Sun's headdress. On earth, it is worn by the headman who, as the human leader, assimilates the celestial powers of the Sun among men.

*Opposite:* **120** A Zoró feather crown headdress with diaphanous white egret feather projections and a central diadem of scarlet macaw plumes ending in white feather finials. This elegant headdress shows the refined aesthetic of juxtaposing the filmy white basal plumes with the darker, uniform long plumes above. The white weighted tips of the latter recapitulate the white body below and bob to meet that filmy mass in movement.

# Body Decoration: Marked for Life ——

For lowland South Amerindians, the body is not a biological given, unfolding mechanically as programmed by the genetic code, as we Westerners imagine it. Rather, it is a fragile and fleeting fortress of culture carefully and tenuously constructed from natural materials, and capable of returning to the wilds in illness and death. One constructs oneself just as one actively builds others – by using the materials and ordering principles of nature. This building activity begins in lowland ethno-physiological theories that not only state you can be "a little pregnant," but also that a child may have "plural fathers"; and, in fact, one doesn't need a woman at all to give birth. These theories are based on logical inferences from observable facts: certain substances enter the body and others leave it; semen goes in and a fetus comes out. From this one can logically assume, as many lowlanders do, that males actively construct the fetuses of children in the passive wombs of hollow women. Since the fetus is thus a growing and congealing ball of male ejaculate, young couples work vigorously at "building" the infant up until its birth, and a woman's multiple male sex partners must acknowledge their shared paternity (extramarital affairs are common in the lowlands and highly institutionalized, although not without the risk of jealousy).

Of course, rather than proclaiming masculine power, this male appropriation of gestation is really a species of womb envy that does not stop at birth. While the child is nursing it is linked to women and remains in their domain until puberty. At that time, the boy is ripped out of his maternal context; he may go to a central men's hut to live and, in any case, he is ceremonially given rebirth by men who oversee his rite of passage. If women give birth naturally, men will assert that they give rebirth culturally. Thus the various forms of corporeal decoration, body modeling and mutilation that constitute the emblematic style of each tribe take the form of a "social skin" added to one's biological skin.[42] It has even been shown that among the Suyá the size, color and class of body adornments (lower-lip plugs versus penis sheaths) reflect the ethos of the group.[43] For a young boy intent on receiving instruction from his elders, his ear plugs will symbolize that receptivity just as his growing lip plug will highlight the adult assertiveness of village elders haranguing their followers. Meanwhile, more aggressive and faction-prone village groups like the Kayapó will signal their bellicosity (while asserting they seek to contain it) by not wearing large ear plugs (they do not listen to others well, deafened by the pursuit of individual and group advancement), by sporting exaggerated lip plugs, thereby signaling their oral assertiveness, and by wearing penis sheaths, marking the need to constrain their phallic aggressiveness.

Body modeling, such as the Shipibo practice of frontal-occipital skull deformation which yields an elegantly sloping forehead, marks people's ethnic status for life. On the other hand, body mutilations, like the filing of incisors to emulate the pointed canines of jaguars on the Ecuadorian coast, hint at permanent emulation of admired natural symbols. But not all bodily mutilation is targeted at males in the lowlands. The radical clitoridectomy of Shipibo maidens before marriage is the ceremonial re-enactment of the masculine

**Opposite**
**121–3 Body ornaments.**
*Top:* A man's toucan-feather belt, from the Urubú-Kaapor. *Center:* Feathered armbands made by the Nambikwara. *Bottom:* A pair of Kayapó-Kreen Akrore men's ear plugs made of freshwater mother-of-pearl and red *urucu*-dyed cotton and wood.

ideology about primordial Amazons who must be castrated so that men will remain the unique owners of the phallus and the dominators of women.

Lastly, reversible and mutable body "masks" such as those provided by body painting provide the visual text by which a person's sexual status, mood or motivation can be read. A man will paint himself (and his hunting dog) red to ensure success in the hot blood of the hunt with the same logic that he will paint himself black in the deadly mask of death before he sets out on a raid. But body painting hints not only at individual mood or intent but also at the cosmic connections of the human physique and health. One observer has shown how the continuous form-line of Shipibo geometric designs painted on face, hands and feet cures by emulating the tissue of connectedness that characterized the healthy union of the Dawn World.[44] Hence ordered body paint, even if it is the invisible skein that the shaman places over the afflicted body in his visions, restores a healthy equilibrium to the ill body and stands as protective armor against the disordered asymmetry of contagion and bewitchment.[45] These patterns covered everything in ancient times, but now they are only visible to the hallucinating shaman, who can put them right.[46]

As Lévi-Strauss pointed out in his early, brilliant study of Mbayá-Caduveo face paint, "mask cultures" are pervasive in the South-American tropics, where an imperturbable surface equanimity hides a turbulent war of emotions that other cultures, such as our own, would wear more openly on their faces. But not all masks are the transparent tracery of face paint:

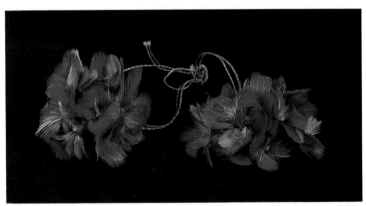

concealing the face and the whole body is also common in lowland dance costumes. This literal masking suggests another contrast between Westerners and Native Americans. Western civilization since the Enlightenment has viewed the empirical world as the only demonstrable reality; in the lowlands the pervasive use of hallucinogenic drugs produces a dualistic world view in which what one sees is not necessarily reality. Like Platonists, South Amerindians conceive of a perfect, hidden, reality behind this perceptible and all-too-imperfect world. That real world can be accessed by altered states of awareness. Humans transform into animals and men put on the masked head-and-body dance costumes of the spirits and thereby become them.

Another hallmark of the sartorial art of lowland South Amerindians, in addition to plumes and body paint, is the numerous ligatures that men and women wrap above their joints. Sometimes they are woven on the body and never cut off until they have rotted and broken, leaving permanent channels in the flesh of their wearers. These ligatures cause the muscles of the biceps and calves to swell unnaturally, thereby, via sympathetic magic, conferring strength and beauty. Indeed, ligatures are the first items given, as talismans, to infants to protect their fragile lives. In the adult they become the woven or beaded wrapping attachment-point for danglers or sprouting feathers. Like the lashed and bound house within which the body dwells, these bindings act as encircling walls and doors closing off the portals of the body.

In cultures such as these, where the body is spiritual as well as physical, the entry and exit of substances and breath is a magically charged and dangerous affair. To be closed or open is to be masculine or feminine respectively, protected from, or subject to, magical aggression—intrusion like the

124 Two polygonal wax and clay-modeled dance masks with palm-frond mantles, called *tamoko*, made by the Wayana-Aparai. They are used during the Cumeeira hut dedication ceremony, and their pointed chins metonymically recall the pointed base of the central house post which is thrust into the ground as the last stage in the hut's completion.

*Opposite:* 125 A Yawalapití jaguar pelt crown with fiber dangler. The placement of a jaguar's pelt at the apex of a man's body accords with the corporeal hierarchy in the lowlands: the jaguar's pelt is never found lower than a headdress band, a cape or a belt. This signifies the supernatural role of the jaguar as mediator between Earth and Sky while also recalling its prowess as a capable climber, and hunter from trees, as well as its home in mountain caves.

blowing curse and the sucking cure. Since one "opens" a body by hacking at its joints, they become analogized to so many portals or eyes into the body. A good shaman can see in X-ray vision into one's body to rip up, suck out, or throw away the invading soul-material. It is in this context that the plethora of encircling body adornments that lowlanders wear makes sense. They are not just cosmetics; like the latticework of body paint, they are armor. Just as the encircled hut is concentrically bound by its lashing "bushrope" vines and the concentric zones of the plaza, house garden, swidden and deep-forest total settlement system, so too is the hut of the body enmeshed in multiple bindings, all concentrically placed, doors within doors.[47]

This system of encircling bindings reveals that the major wrapping ring, worn around a man's waist, frequently his only item of clothing, is his belt. It represents one of his most treasured power and status accoutrements, and was even replicated in stone as a ball-playing trophy in those regions, like the Antilles, where stone was common. In the culturally affiliated Guianas, that central ligature, the belt, is frequently made of the golden furry pelt of the prime masculine

symbol, the jaguar. Jaguar pelts are also worn elsewhere high on a man's body, such as wrapped around his crown. Belts are traded by men to cement social and political ties; they were one of the first Indian "treasures" given to Columbus by the Taíno of the Caribbean – the first gift received by any white man from an Amerindian.

It is this endlessly repeated order that gives unconscious harmony to the world that comprises Amerindian culture. Culture itself, a systematic selection of the rules and elements of a style of living and thinking, is a vast machine for teaching and redundancy. It endlessly repeats, on different levels, and where possible on simultaneous channels, the same messages, like some practiced pedagogue. Thus by the time a member of the tribe has reached adulthood, the artificial culture has become natural, and other forms of life not only unintelligible but also loathsome and subhuman. Ironically, then, what made the Amerindian appear cultured to himself – his plethora of feathered and natural wrapped accoutrements, and therefore his lack of what Westerners regarded as proper clothing – was precisely what made him look savage to his European oppressor.

*This page*
**126 A Waiwai man's woven seed-bead belt with beaded hanging elements ending in macaw breast-feather finial danglers.**

*Opposite*
**Left: 127, 129 Two pairs of feather-fringed (upper) armbands, called *lapu-ruwai-diwa*, from the Urubú-Kaapor. These artifacts can be worn by either men or women.**

**Top, right: 128 A pair of woven cotton (upper) armbands with a regularly overlapping feather covering and cotton string danglers (*padadi*), made by the Rikbaktsá.**

**Bottom, right: 130 A pair of men's feather (upper) armbands, from the Kamayurá tribe. In effect, these feather ring ligatures are shortened "wings" that, like the armbands with projecting plumes worn in the same manner, allow men to "fly" across the village plaza in dance.**

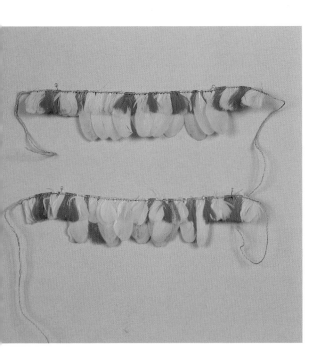

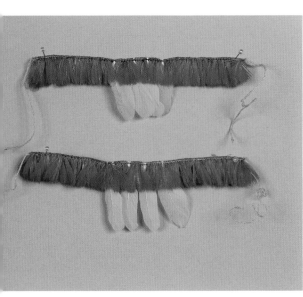

*Opposite:* **131 A Kobeua painted bark-cloth body-mask with attached arms and plaited mantle. These dance costumes are the most complex ensembles currently made in the northwest Amazon. They play a role in initiation ceremonies.**

*This page:* **132 Two *jakui* masks: tall cylindrical basketry feather headdress-body dance costumes with a feather mosaic covering, feather projections and palm-frond danglers. These spirit masks, made by the Tapirapé, are worn by members of the Bird Societies who emerge from the *takana*, or men's hut, during dry-season ceremonies, when they circle the village and sing the songs of their respective bird species. The women give them offerings of soup and the singers return to the *takana* to be followed by other pairs.**

**133**  A Jurúna green parrot-feather crown with a long cotton cape, called an *abeata*. The cotton strands of the cape end in long bird plume danglers. This spectacular headdress is used during the Anai-karia festival of the dead, and can only be worn by the shaman.

**134**  A *bokra*, a conical fiber dance costume mask covered with regularly overlapping feather mosaic designs, with scarlet macaw feather projections and a palm-fiber mantle. Made by the Apinayé tribe, it is worn during the Pad ceremony by men, who dance in pairs.

**135**  An *ime*, a conical bark-cloth dance costume mask with a scarlet macaw plume projection and a fiber mantle, from the Piaroa-Huarime. Originally, the bark cloth was clearly covered by simple painted clay and wax designs.

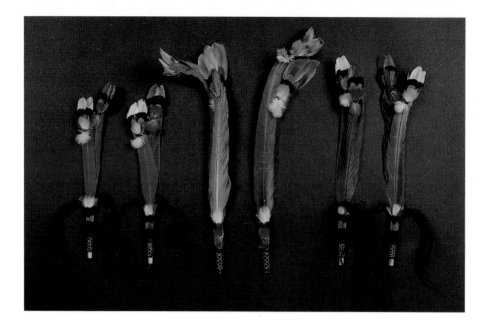

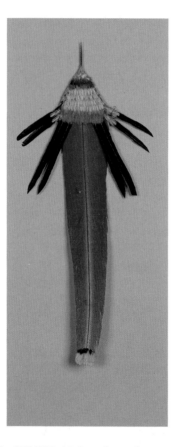

*Top, left:* 136 Rikbaktsá men's scarlet macaw plume nose pins with feather finials (*tsun-doro*).

*Top, right:* 137 A *menaupe*, a man's bandolier, made from glass beads, feathers and nut shells by the Kayapó-Kuben Kran Kein.

*Bottom, left:* 138 A *rembe-pipo*, a man's scarlet macaw and hummingbird feather labret worn during the name-giving ceremonies of the Urubú-Kaapor tribe.

*Bottom, right:* 139 An Urubú-Kaapor woman's wrapped comb with blue and yellow macaw breast-feather streamers, called a *kiwaw-putir*. These combs are made by men for their women, but may sometimes also be worn by the men themselves.

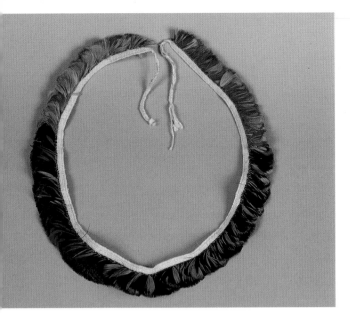

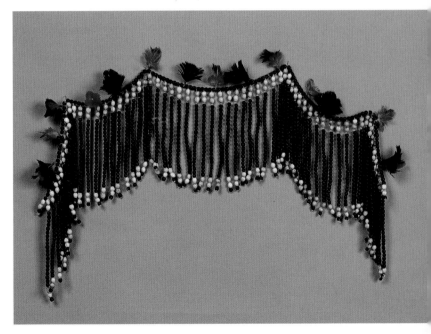

*Top, left:* 140 An Urubú-Kaapor man's feather-fringed belt (*diwa-kuawhar*).

*Top, right:* 141 A man's glass-beaded belt with *tapir* hooves and gourd danglers, from the Kayapó-Kreen Akrore tribe.

*Center:* 142 A Mehinaku man's woven glass bead belt with decorative panels depicting the Brazilian flag. It is worn only during specific ceremonies, such as the Huka-Huka, the wrestling matches performed during the Kuarup festival.

*Bottom, left:* 143 A blue-and-yellow macaw-feather skirt made by the Guajajara tribe. The feathers are literally woven into the cotton frame of the skirt.

*Bottom, right:* 144 An Urubú-Kaapor woman's seed-beaded hip string with feather danglers.

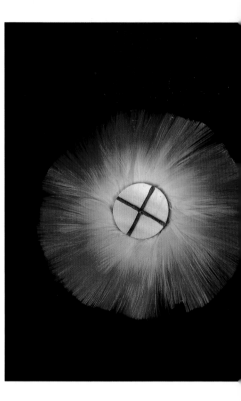

Many of these ear plugs illustrate the bizarre, but visually compelling, combination of disparate natural forms found in lowland body ornaments.

*Top, far left:* 145 A pair of rosette ear plugs with radial toucan-feather projections, from the Nambikwara tribe.

*Top, left:* 146 A pair of man's ear plugs with freshwater mother-of-pearl centers and breast-feather radial projections, made by the Shambioa. The "X"-elements in the center are painted wax. These ear plugs are frequently traded to the neighboring Karajá.

*Bottom, far left:* 147 A pair of woman's ear plugs with peccary-tusk centers and radial macaw-feather projections, made by the Karajá. These gleaming white peccary tusks encased in a circlet of bright feathers show that white teeth are variants of shiny freshwater pearl and other reflective materials.

*Bottom, left:* 148 A pair of three-strand green iridescent beetle wing casing ear ornaments with toucan-feather danglers, made by the Aguaruna. In addition to their iridescent properties, these stiff wing casings also function as rattles, clattering as their wearer dances or even turns his head.

*Above:* 149 A pair of feathered ear danglers, from the Paressí tribe.

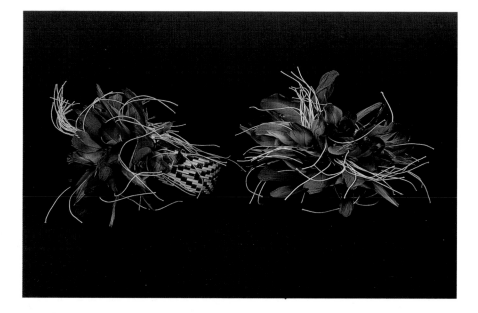

*Top:* **150** A pair of men's woven fiber (upper) armbands with regularly overlapping feather coverings and cotton string danglers, from the Kayapó-Xikrin.

*Center:* **152** A pair of twill-weave basketry cylindrical (upper) armbands with macaw and parrot feather and nut danglers, also from the Kayapó-Xikrin.

*Bottom:* **153** A pair of *urucu*-red woven cotton cuffs with string danglers, made by the Karajá tribe. In parts of the Guianas, as among the Cariban Wayana, these fiber cuffs have been replaced by shiny metal cuffs in historic times.

*Above:* **151** A man's howler-monkey fur (upper) armband with multiple toucan tail danglers, made by the Yanomamö.

*Above:* 154 A Yanomamö man's curassow head-pelt (upper) armband with parrot-wing danglers.

*Right:* 155 A pair of woven cotton (upper) armbands with bird wing bone and yellow and blue macaw-feather danglers, made by the Rikbaktsá tribe.

# 7 Art as Performance

The construction and reconstruction of the self – the cultural person, not the modern, anonymous individual – reaches a multimedia apotheosis in ceremonies where myth, oration, dance, music, sartorial and corporeal art, architecture and the organization of private and public space make of life the stuff of performance and theatre.

We have failed to understand feather and other art because we haven't seen it functioning in ceremonies, where it comes to life. Only recently has this begun to change, perhaps because of the increased use of 16mm cameras and now video. The feather crowns shown here, for instance, have long arching plumes weighted with resin finials so that they bounce when the wearer dances. His silent seed and teeth-shell danglers clatter into life as rattles when the Cariban Wayana man from French Guiana and Surinam performs during the ant-shield ceremony. While the spidery framework of feather attachments weaves and bobs above his head, he plays a feather-encased flute and his stamping feet beat a rhythm on a wooden-plank earth drum laid over a trench as his whole being resonates like a one-man-band of kinesthetic visual and aural performance. Simple in isolation, lowland arts come alive and achieve their true complexity in performance. Performance studies are only beginning among us, so we may yet catch up to the Indians.

These performances, and the mythic world they summon, illuminate otherwise enigmatic artifacts. For example, the elaborate wasp or ant shields of the Wayana-Aparai, of which there are several examples in the Mekler collection, are woven into profile images of animals or fish, usually

carnivorous species like the jaguar and the piranha. Thus they symbolize the strength that the young boy must acquire at his puberty ceremony so that he can become a man, a warrior, be heard in council and take a wife. If he successfully passes this ordeal he will keep the shield (*kunana*) as a trophy.

The double-headed wasp shield (ill. 162) represents a monstrous snake-jaguar that arches through the sky, its curved body ending in two plumed heads. The plumes adorning this shield symbolize the hair or feathers (the same term is used for both body coverings) on the body and head of the supernaturally flying snake-jaguar which the Waiwai, the Wayana's western Carib cousins, call Urufiri, a cannibalistic Master of Designs whose jaguar pelt was used to instruct the first Indians in the art of twill-weaving baskets. This flying Dragon is none other than the Plumed Serpent found widely from the Guianas to Mesoamerica, and represents a rainbow demon. Therefore, this shield symbolizes not only the bravery of the young man who endures without screaming or flinching the bites of its "teeth," but also the mastery of the basketry arts which he must possess to fully attain manhood.

During the pre- and early contact eras, the Carib were notable for their warlike tendencies, and the male puberty rite fostered useful virtues like bravery and stoicism. The ant and wasp shields, the feather headdresses and the associated musical instruments are part of a ceremony that lasts twenty-four hours and sorely tests the endurance of the initiates. It takes place in the cleared dance plaza in front of the men's hut and begins in the forest with the shaman and his helpers constructing the elaborate spidery headdresses and dance

costumes out of cane frameworks and bright macaw, toucan and curassow feathers which have been carefully stored in bamboo tubes and plaited baskets.

At dawn on the first day three or four initiates gather in the central plaza under the direction of the shaman, clutching their dance arrows in their right hand (their hollow flutes, with their feminine connotations,[48] are grasped in their left hands). The young boys have come from the surrounding feminine periphery, from their mother's hearths, and are destined, if successful, to leave the world of women forever and move toward the center of the plaza and the men's hut in its middle.[49] They partake of food that has been specially prepared for them by their mothers as a parting gift, and then dance non-stop for the whole day, into the night and well into the next morning, all without food or drink.[50] Meanwhile, the shaman and his helpers have collected large wasps which have been made comatose with tobacco smoke and insert up to one hundred of them in each of the small rectangular woven panels in the center of the shields. The rest of the shields' surfaces are covered in a colorful feather mosaic, making these some of the most beautiful and elaborate artifacts produced by lowlanders. Then, at nightfall, the shaman strikes the shields against a house post and shakes them vigorously to awaken the enraged wasps. The boys, wearied from an entire day of dancing, hungry and thirsty, step forward one at a time and the shaman applies the shield to their chest, arms and back (and frequently to their thighs and calves as well; five or six places in all). The young men stoically raise their arms, allowing themselves to be stung without resistance.

**157** A conical feather headdress-body dance costume with twin scarlet macaw plume projections, feather finials, and a fiber mantle. Made by the Tirío tribe, Guianan highlands.

**158** A Tirío man's tall cylindrical basketry crown-body dance costume (*saipa*) with a feather mosaic covering and scarlet macaw-feather and white down-covered cane frame projections. It is closely related to the neighboring Wayana *orok* headdress (ill. 10). The spidery, feather-encrusted framework of this dance costume has great torsional flexibility; it twists, bobs and weaves as the dancer goes through his steps, conferring a vibrant kinetic aspect to this (now static) headdress.

159  A Tirío tall, cylindrical man's basketry
crown with a feather mosaic covering, feather
projections and cotton danglers. The long,
arching lateral macaw plumes are weighted
down with small feathers appended with latex
glue. They bob up and down as the dancer
moves.

*Opposite*

**Wayana-Aparai animal effigy ant shields (kunana). The feathers are glued in large blocks of color onto basketry frames in the form of real and imaginary animals. After fire ants or wasps are applied to these panels during the ant-shield ceremony, the shields are pressed against the male initiates' bodies. If a boy cannot endure the excruciating pain of the insect stings, he cannot become a man. This ordeal is also thought to impart valor in war, stoicism and energy to perform arduous tasks.**

*Top, left:* **160 A fish-effigy ant shield, probably representing the piranha, which can reduce a hapless swimming mammal to bones in seconds.**

*Top, right:* **161 This kunana probably represents the spider monkey, which is noted for its big canines. Although actually a vegetarian, it often plays the role of a Forest Ogre in lowland mythology.**

*Bottom:* **162. A double-headed plumed dragon (jaguar) effigy kunana. This devouring compound monster is based on a hybrid jaguar-anaconda-caterpillar. Inverted, it forms the "plumed serpent" of Guianan and Central American mythology, the shimmering rainbow dragon whose dual heads are buried in the earth.**

They are not permitted to flinch or scream. Those who do or, even worse, who faint in toxic shock, must undergo the rite again if they hope to become men. An alternative practice is to secure huge, solitary hunting ants[51] and weave their heads and thoraxes into the shields. These ants carry an even more venomous charge than their wasp cousins possess. Their stings are not just excruciatingly painful; they also are thought to inject a charge of energy and strength into the young men's bodies. Indeed, in former times, even warriors long past this rite of passage regularly resorted to the ant ordeal before a battle, just as modern Indians do before a major period of physical exertion, such as tree-felling.

Then, as a reward for their suffering, the triumphant young men are permitted to put on the elaborate feather headdresses, with their projecting finials of scarlet macaw plumes, and dance with them before their mothers and other women, thus publicly confirming their new status as men, warriors, and potential husbands. In the past, this headdress was the central element in the paraphernalia of those two hyper-males, the war chief and the shaman. It is the most impressive of all Guianan headdresses, with its cosmically stacked rings of (from top to bottom) harpy, macaw, toucan and curassow feathered mosaics covering the cylindrical core and forming fret-like designs, evocative of the jaguar and other super predators.

As the Wayana wasp- or ant-shield ceremony demonstrates, many Amazonian artifacts have a kinetic function; they are meant to come alive when they are used or displayed in public performance. Pots have hidden false bottoms in which clay pellets have been molded; they rattle when the proffered beer is quaffed. Water bottles whistle when the water they contain is poured; channels are formed in rims of other vessels for the flow of liquids; and stirrup-spout handles become similar conduits of flowing water. Designs are painted with reversible (anatropic) imagery so that when artifacts are inverted in dance, different designs or representations greet the audience. Double, Janus-headed images prevail, so that when dancers turn their backs they are still "facing" you, but with a different visage. Positive-negative designs project multiple images.

All of these bobbing, whistling, stamping, bellowing, shaking, transforming objects, themselves inexplicable except for their function in ceremonies or placement on the human body in motion, move in carefully orchestrated dance on special stages of the village or the communal hut. Shakespeare was right, all the world is indeed a stage – of visible (public) and invisible (private) areas where action unfolds. Ceremonies are the original happenings and even leave ephemeral art behind, to be consumed by its own production. For example, the Shipibo had a special kind of earth-design dance in which the steps of the dancers as they moved across the carefully swept plaza formed intricate geometric patterns, only to be obliterated by the prancing feet of the dancers as they retraced their steps.

If the befeathered dancer is the player, then the hut in which he lives and the village in which he parades is the stage.[52] The central plaza is a male space where public activities such as dances unfold. (If a man spends too much time behind the hut in the women's area where the refuse is swept, he is in danger of being labeled a feminine "trash-yard man.") Then, encircling the village are the house garden and latrine areas, filled with snaking paths where adulterous lovers meet in trysting areas. The next layer out is represented by secondary growth and the women's gardens, surrounded in turn by the deep or gallery forests into which men roam, to hunt or to make war, and women are prohibited to venture unaccompanied.

The organization of space is also concentric within the hut: the peripheral wall-less apartments of the communal hut with their slung hammocks are the feminine region while the central region is the masculine area where shamanism and rituals are staged. Thus just as tasks alternate by sex, so too are they accomplished in sex-typed spaces that alternate concentrically outward from the center. If men determine any sequence by initiating the activity (before women can garden men must cut the trees for slash-and-burn horticulture; before women can cook, men must hunt, etc.), then priority in time becomes analogous to centrality in space, and male areas begin the concentric zones by occupying the center of the hut in the center of the village.

It is in the plaza that the most impressive lowland artifacts are presented: the full-body masked dance costumes worn by men. They are brought to this cleared space from either the central men's hut or ceremonial house, the area of culture, or from the surrounding forest and rivers, the realms of nature. When they come from the center, the men's hut, the masked dancers represent the rules of culture and the massed choreography of adherence to those rules. In contrast, when they shamble in from the forest or are "fished up" from the rivers, these dancers represent the principle of individualized chaos, illness, death, accusations of witchcraft and rumor-mongering, physical violence and murder. The huge mask and body costume found among the Kamayurá of the Upper Xingú, for example, originates in the water, but ends its life in the men's hut in the middle of the village, where it is kept until it rots away.

The most elaborate masks and body costumes south of the Amazon are found in the Xingú culture area where peace reigns and groups pertaining to all of the major language families of Brazil exist in harmony, many in single tribal villages. Through systematic inter-village visiting and trading these groups have evolved a common regional culture called Xinguano. Many of the masks, for example, are shared or play tribal variations on region-wide themes.[53] Some groups, like the Mehinaku, fabricate the masks out of wood with a *buriti* palm raffia skirt, which hides the body of the dancer, while others like the Kalapálo make their masks out of materials as diverse as gourds, basketry and old hammocks. All of these masks are ephemeral; they are constructed only for the purpose of the ceremony and then allowed to disintegrate.

The masks are brightly painted in red, white and black, colors which contrast with the dull grayish-brown of their raffia skirts, the dull red of the baked clay dance plaza and the uniform gray and green of the surrounding huts and vegetation. Their brightness signals danger and, indeed, they are armed with sharp dogfish or piranha teeth and therefore project an aggressive, but also protective, demeanor.[54] They possess exaggerated features because the powerful beings they embody are viewed as being intensely alive, what one student of the Kalapálo has aptly termed "hyperanimacy,"[55] a process of communication with humans that takes place in the medium of music and movement. Indeed, the freshwater mother-of-pearl eyes of the masks flash the powers of creative transformation that only powerful spirit beings can bring to humans.

Generally, these masks are not combined with feathers, which have the same flashing powers of animation, except when they refer to flying supernaturals, in which case they have trailers of feathers streaming down their backs. When humans dance without these masks, however, they put on their own "masks" of red body paint and feathers. The Kamayurá mask pictured on page 107 (ill. 172) is an exception to that rule of complementary distribution between feathers and masks, for it sprouts three tall

scarlet macaw tail plumes from its square head, perhaps in expression of the wealth of the family that commissions it. The entire costume weighs over one hundred pounds and takes days or even weeks to create. The shaman must don it and dance for three days to summon the spirits of the lake to cure an illness.

Another Xingú mask that summons the water does so not for the curing of illness but the "curing" of the social disease of rumor-mongering, which is equally essential for the functioning of society. It is a Kalapálo water-spirit mask that is metaphorically "fished out" of the water, an element linked with women and dangerous sex, at the end of a ceremony of insult. Unlike the songs in other Kalapálo ceremonies, which are sung less for their content than for their melody and rhythm and as a sign of village harmony, the songs here are more shouted than sung, usually into the faces of purported rumor-mongers by the accused (the former often women, the latter men) acting in a cacophony of individual visits to the various huts of the village. The goal is to externalize in performance all the nasty things said about one behind one's back in normal daily life by singing them before the people who have been spreading the stories, which frequently involve accusations of witchcraft leading to expulsion from the village. The rumor-mongers may, in turn, take umbrage and douse the dancers with ashes or *piqui* fruit mash. After venting these feelings in a socially condoned public setting, the village may once again don its social mask of equanimity as the sponsors of the ceremony call the masked dancers from the water.[56]

Such social control, even if it is the venting of pent-up hostilities, as in the case of the Kalapálo dance costume mask, is central to masking in South America as it is to this phenomenon in comparative perspective. A set of Mekranoti masked dance

**164–70 Masks.** *Opposite, left:* Two Kayapó anteater conical painted fiber dance costume masks with plaited horizontal tube arms, a projecting tube mouth and a palm-fiber mantle. The Mekranoti man's *patkaro* mask *(top)* is part of the Koko ceremony that interrupts the women's Bijok ceremony. Armed with a piranha mandible, the dancer attempts to scratch and discipline the women's children. *Center:* This is the Xikrin version of the Mekranoti mask, above, called a *tamandua*. *Bottom:* A rectangular wooden dance costume mask painted with a fish motif, made by the Mehinaku. It has a palm-fiber mantle and lateral palm-fiber projections.

*Opposite, center right:* A *guariba*, a pillow-shaped, painted fiber dance costume mask with a palm-fiber mantle, Kayapó-Kuben Kran Kein tribe. This mask dances with the anteater mask, providing comic relief like the similar howler monkey masks of the Mekranoti. *Opposite, far right and bottom, and this page, above:* Three Kamayurá dance costume masks used to evoke the fish spirits during the dry season and therefore insure plentiful fishing: a painted, rectangular, wooden carved dance costume mask with a palm-fiber mantle; and two painted burlap-cloth dance costume masks – one conical, the other oval – with palm-fiber mantles.

*Captions for 171–2 overleaf.*

All of these Kayapó feather hoop headdresses are worn on the back, suspended from the forehead by a tump-line. Their feathers radiate from a channeled and bowed split-cane frame. Among the largest "headdresses" in all the lowlands, these examples of feather art form a nimbus for the whole upper body of the dancers who cargo them. Generically called *meoko*, they are all employed in name-giving ceremonies.

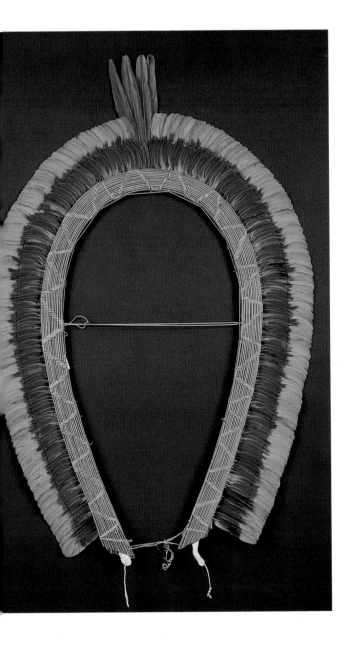

*From left to right*
173  A yellow *oropendola* feather headdress worn by the Kayapó-Txukahamae.

174–5  Two Kayapó-Mekranoti headdresses with central scarlet macaw plume projections.

176  This Kayapó-Xikrin *meoko* headdress has concentric raptor feather aureoles.

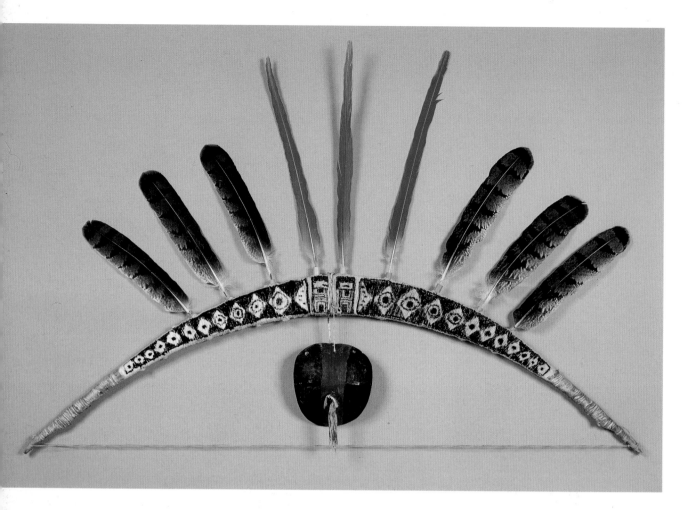

**177** A Kamayurá bow-shaped headdress with single harpy-eagle plume projections flanking three scarlet macaw plumes (*awarau*). The frame of the bow is wrapped with cotton string and painted with *genipa* in black diamond designs. A painted half-gourd "mask" is suspended beneath the bow. This headdress is used during the new hut consecration ceremony and then hung within the hut for good luck.

**178** A man's toucan-feather headband with porcupine quill danglers, made by the Achuara.

*Opposite*
**179** A *krokroti*, a dorsal feather hoop headdress on a bowed split-cane frame, with a scarlet macaw and blue and yellow macaw plume projection. It is employed by the Kayapó-Xikrin during name-giving ceremonies.

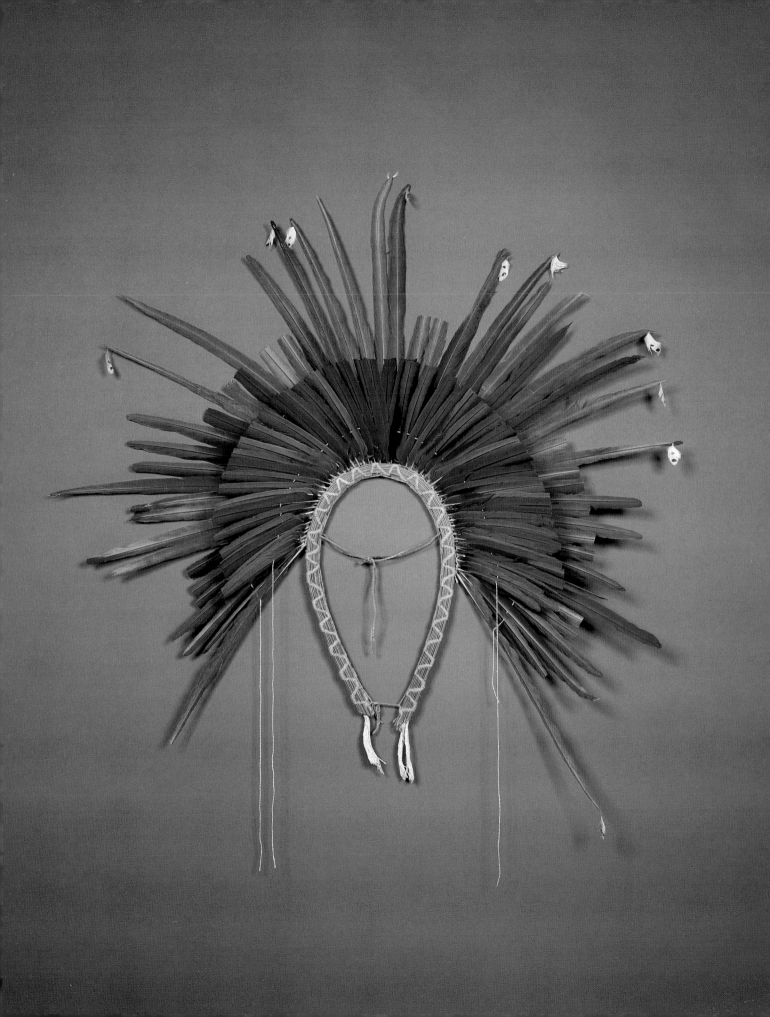

*Below:* **180 A Karajá radial headdress with a split-cane bow frame covered with wax and white clay paint, called a *Iurina*. It is composed of white egret feathers, with central scarlet and lateral blue-and-yellow macaw plume projections.**

*Right:* **181 A back ornament with a hanging plume fringe, made by the Gaviao tribe. While there is an emphasis on frontality in lowland feather art, this back ornament reminds us that dancers are also meant to be seen from the back as they pirouette before their audiences.**

*Opposite*
**182 A feather crown headdress with scarlet macaw feather projections, made by the Trumaí tribe in the Xingú region.**

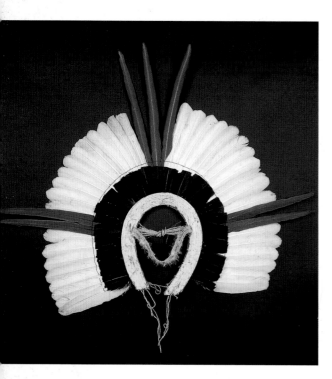

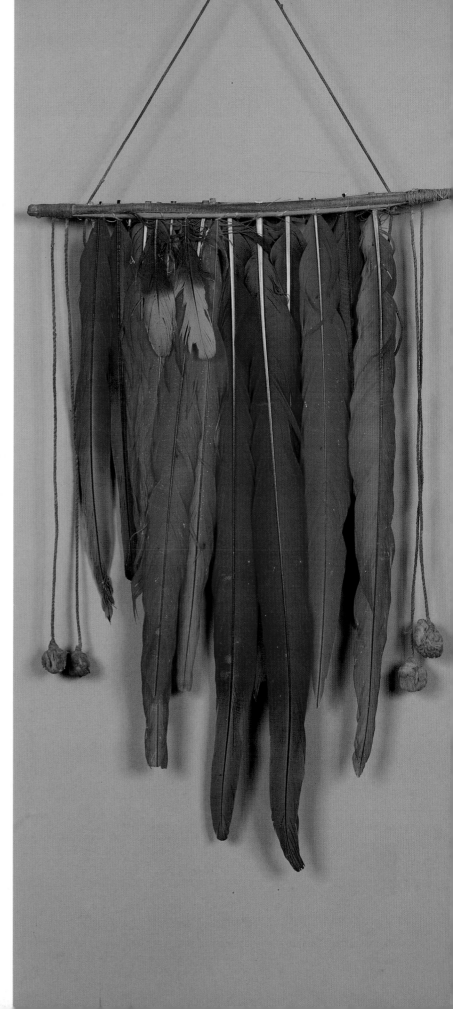

*Opposite*
**183 A *lori-lori* feather cap headdress with a central feather projection. The feathers that compose this very traditional Karajá headdress are imbricated into an extremely loose netted fiber foundation.**

*This page*
**184 A Kayapó-Txukahamae dorsal feather headdress with a central plume projection. This traditional headdress resembles the Karajá *lori-lori*, opposite, but has a much tighter woven foundation.**

185 A Karajá feather cap headaddress with a central feather projection. This is the old-fashioned version of the *lori-lori*, where the body of the cap is fashioned from complex feather rosettes rather than simpler imbricated feather mosaic.

186 A *lori-lori*, a Karajá feather cap headaddress with feather danglers.

**187** A unique Kalapálo cap headdress constructed of a tight fiber cap surmounted by a gourd and another, inverted tight fiber cap out of which sprouts a scarlet macaw plume projection. As the straight lateral projections above the gourd suggest arms, this headdress may represent an abstract human figure.

# Map of the Amazon region

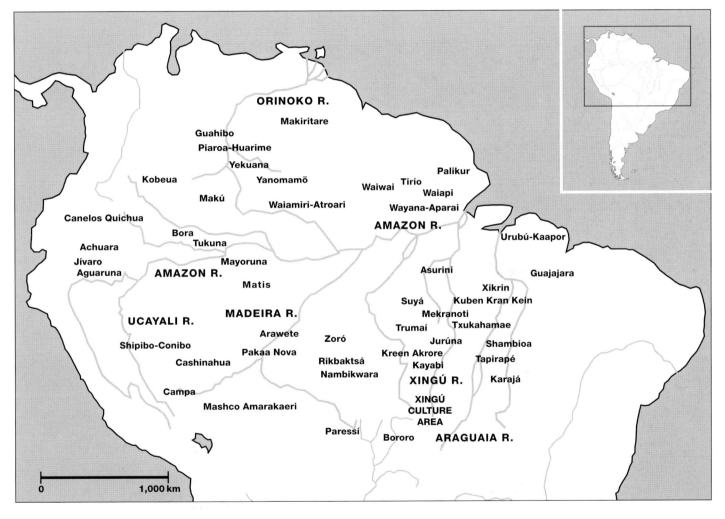

ORINOKO R.

Makiritare

Guahibo

Piaroa-Huarime

Yekuana

Kobeua

Yanomamö

Palikur

Makú

Waiwai

Tirío

Waiapi

Waiamiri-Atroari

Wayana-Aparai

Canelos Quichua

AMAZON R.

Urubú-Kaapor

Bora

Tukuna

Achuara

Mayoruna

Jívaro

Asurini

Guajajara

Aguaruna

AMAZON R.

Xikrin

Matis

Suyá

Kuben Kran Kein

Mekranoti

UCAYALI R.

MADEIRA R.

Trumaí

Txukahamae

Arawete

Zoró

Jurúna

Shambioa

Shipibo-Conibo

Pakaa Nova

Kreen Akrore

Tapirapé

Cashinahua

Rikbaktsá

Kayabi

Nambikwara

Karajá

Campa

XINGÚ R.

Mashco Amarakaeri

XINGÚ
CULTURE
AREA

Paressí

Bororo

ARAGUAIA R.

0    1,000 km

XINGÚ CULTURE AREA

Kalapálo
Kamayurá
Kuikúru
Mehinaku
Txikao
Waurá
Yawalapití

# Notes on the text

1. Paradoxically, this incredible profusion of life subsists on a virtually sterile substratum. See Michael Goulding, *Amazon–The Flooded Forest* (BBC Books, London, 1989), p. 202.

2. Roland W. Bergman, *Amazon Economics: The Simplicity of Shipibo Indian Wealth* (University Microfilms International, Ann Arbor, 1980), p. 49.

3. See Jens Yde, *Material Culture of the Waiwai* (National Museum of Denmark, Copenhagen, 1965).

4. See Betty J. Meggers, *Amazonia: Man and Culture in a Counterfeit Paradise* (Aldine, Chicago, 1971).

5. See José Toribio Medina (ed.), *The Discovery of the Amazon* (Dover Publications, New York, 1988).

6. See Anna Curtenius Roosevelt, *Moundbuilders of the Amazon: Geophysical Archaeology on Marajó Island, Brazil* (Academic Press, New York, 1991).

7. This argument is based on still relatively limited research in a very difficult area. It generalizes over a vast region and will doubtless be refined as we know more about local sequences. Moreover, the major figures in this debate have modified their positions considerably. For example, a comparison between Roosevelt's first book, *Parmana, Prehistoric Maize and Manioc Subsistence Along the Amazon and Orinoco* (Academic Press, New York, 1980), and her recent volume, 1991, op. cit., a collaboration with Brazilian colleagues, shows her transition from a materialistic, environmentally deterministic treatment of the lowlands, indebted to the approach of Betty Meggers, to a reconstruction recalling that of Donald Lathrap and his students like Joanne Magalis Harris.

8. Compare, for example, the Amazon with its 1,300 species to the Mississippi, with a drainage area almost as large as the Congo, and its 250 species. Tyson R. Roberts points this out in "Ecology of Fishes in the Amazon and Congo Basins," in Betty J. Meggers, Edward S. Ayensu and W. Donald Duckworth (eds.), *Tropical Forest Ecosystems in Africa and South America: A Comparative Review* (Smithsonian Institution Press, Washington, D.C., 1973), p. 240.

9. Donald W. Lathrap, Donald Collier and Helen Chandra, *Ancient Ecuador: Culture, Clay and Creativity 3000–300 B.C.* (Field Museum of Natural History, Chicago, 1975), pp. 22, 30.

10. See Peter G. Roe, *The Cosmic Zygote: Cosmology in the Amazon Basin* (Rutgers University Press, New Brunswick, 1982).

11. Gerardo Reichel-Dolmatoff, *Beyond the Milky Way: Hallucinatory Imagery of the Tukano Indians* (University of California, Los Angeles, 1978), p. 149.

12. Thomas Gregor, *Mehinaku: The Drama of Daily Life in a Brazilian Indian Village* (University of Chicago Press, Chicago, 1977), pp. 35, 38.

13. Peter G. Roe, "Of Rainbow Dragons and the Origins of Designs: The Waiwai *Urufiri* and the Shipibo *Ronin ëhua*." *Latin American Indian Literatures Journal*, vol. 5, no. 1 (1989), pp. 1–67.

14. Niels Fock, *Waiwai: Religion and Society of an Amazonian Tribe* (National Museum, Copenhagen, 1963), p. 92, n.5.

15. Daniel Schoepf, *L'art de la plume brésil* (Musée d'Ethnographie, Geneva, 1985), pp. 84–5.

16. Donald W. Lathrap, *The Upper Amazon* (Thames and Hudson, London, and Praeger, New York, 1970), p. 182.

17. Bergman, op. cit., p. 204.

18. Marc de Civrieux, *Watunna: An Orinoco Creation Cycle*, ed. and trans. David M. Guss (North Point Press, San Francisco, 1980), p. 136.

19. Angelika Gebhart-Sayer, *The Cosmos Encoiled: Indian Art of the Peruvian Amazon* (The Americas Society, New York, 1984), p. 7, and Roe, 1989, op. cit.

20. Anthony Seeger, "What Can We Learn When They Sing? Vocal Genres of the Suyá Indians of Central Brazil." *Journal of the Society for Ethnomusicology*, vol. 23 (1979), p. 379.

21. Claude Lévi-Strauss, *Structural Anthropology* (Doubleday/Anchor Books, Garden City, 1967), pp. 253, 255.

22. Helen Tanner, "Cashinahua Weaving," in Jane P. Dwyer (ed.), *The Cashinahua of Eastern Peru* (The Haffenreffer Museum of Anthropology, Brown University, Bristol, 1975), pp. 120, 123.

23. Susan G. Ferguson, "Craftsmanship and Design in Cashinahua Ceramics," in Dwyer (ed.), ibid., p. 127.

24. Terrence Turner, "Commentary: Ethno-Ethnohistory: Myth and History in Native South American Representations of Contact with Western Society," in Jonathan D. Hill (ed.), *Rethinking History and Myth: Indigenous South American Perspectives on the Past* (University of Illinois Press, Urbana, 1988), pp. 243–6.

25. Peter G. Roe, "The Josho Nahuanbo Are All Wet and Undercooked: Shipibo Views of the Whiteman and the Incas in Myth, Legend and History," in Hill (ed.), op. cit.

26. Dorothea S. and Norman E. Whitten, Jr., *From Myth to Creation: Art From Amazonian Ecuador* (University of Illinois Press, Urbana, 1988), pp. 35, 48.

27. Warren R. DeBoer, "Interaction, Imitation, and Communication as Expressed in Style: The Ucayali Experience," in Margaret W. Conkey and Christine A. Hastorf (eds.), *The Uses of Style in Archaeology*, pp. 82–104 (Cambridge University Press, Cambridge and New York, 1990), p. 86.

28. See Gebhart-Sayer, op. cit.

29. This was produced from two sources: *cauxí*, on the Lower Amazon, and *cariapé* on the Upper Amazon and the Guianas. *Cauxí* is produced by wandering through the flooded forest after the waters have receded and plucking freshwater sponges from the branches of trees where they have been stranded. The sponges are burnt and their ash sifted to be added as temper to the ceramic paste. *Cariapé* produces the same effect but is derived from a deciduous tree bark which is burnt, ground in a rocker mortar and added as ash to the clay.

30. José Ortega y Gasset, *The Dehumanization of Art and Other Writings on Art and Culture* (Doubleday & Company, Garden City, 1956), p. 12.

31. David M. Guss, *To Weave and To Sing: Art, Symbol, and Narrative In the South American Rain Forest* (The University of California Press, Berkeley and Los Angeles, 1989), p. 72.

32. Ibid., pp. 81–2.

33. Inside the basket are 80 or 90 pounds of tubers and firewood from the garden and perched on top of the load, a child. Even other animals analogically burdened by their own "loads," like the armadillo and her casque, are transformed primordial women who, in attempting to climb to the masculine heavens on a ladder of arrows made by the Magical Twins, broke it, fell to earth and turned into scuttling edentates, destined to root, like women with their digging sticks, in the earth.

34. Even its shape and technique serve as a defining stigmata of competing ethnic groups. See Dolores Newton, "The Timbira Hammock as a Cultural Indicator of Social Boundaries," in Miles Richardson (ed.), *The Human Mirror: Material and Spatial Images of Man* (Louisiana State University Press, Baton Rouge, 1974), pp. 231–51.

35. Fock, op. cit., p. 42.

36. Greg Urban and Janet Wall Hendricks, "Signal Functions of Masking in Amerindian Brazil." *Semiotica*, vol. 47, nos. 1–4 (1983), pp. 181–216.

37. See Thomas Gregor, *Anxious Pleasures: The Sexual Lives of an Amazonian People* (The University of Chicago Press, Chicago and London, 1985).

38. This information derives from Charles Wagley, *Welcome of Tears: The Tapirapé Indians of Central Brazil* (Oxford University Press, New York, 1977, pp. 108–10), with some of my own comparative perspective. The extraordinary variety of feather colors in the various specimens of these masks in the Mekler collection may be a response to feather shortages of specific birds caused by over-production of masks. Wagley reports how by 1965 these masks were being mass-produced in the men's hut for sale to museums and collectors; in one plate he pictures an artisan carving one specimen while above him hang five unfinished *upé*. (The *upé* in my personal collection, although correct in every other manner, substitutes dyed chicken feathers for the no-longer-obtainable raptor and macaw tail feathers.) Some of the variant colors may also result from acculturative influences such as the Brazilian flag or the color preferences of the neighboring Kayapó and Karajá who, once enemies, now often become spectators for the dance ceremonies. Indeed, Wagley notes that since the masks used to represent the triumphs of the Tapirapé against these very groups, the Tapirapé now just whisper the mask's real names to avoid agitating their old enemies, now guests. With that non-combative behavior in mind we may understand why more recent authorities argue that the pacified Tapirapé have changed their explanation for these figures and now suggest that they merely commemorate their own dead rather than killed enemies.

39. Among the Mehinaku, also of the Xingú culture area, bull-roarers are decorated after they are carved; they are not considered dangerous for the women, but once they are decorated they become alive and must be fed. Failure to feed them is thought to cause the women's hair to fall out. This illustrates how designs must be incorporated into artifacts before they are considered finished, and thus "awaken" to their functions.

40. Catherine Howard, "Fragments of the Heavens: Feathers as Ornaments Among the Waiwai," in Ruben E. Reina and Kenneth M. Kensinger (eds.), *The Gift of Birds: Featherwork of Native South American Peoples* (The University Museum of Archaeology and Anthropology, University of Pennsylvania, Philadelphia, 1991), p. 56, and Peter G. Roe, "The Language of the Plumes: 'Implicit Mythology' in Shipibo, Cashinahua and Waiwai Feather Adornments," in Mary H. Preuss (ed.), *L.A.I.L. Speaks! Selected Papers From the Seventh International Symposium, Albuquerque, 1989* (Labyrinthos Press, Culver City, CA, 1990), pp. 105–36, pls. A–F.

41. Roe, 1989, op. cit., fig. 3.

42. Terrence Turner, "Cosmetics: The Language of Bodily Adornment," in James P. Spradley and David W. McCurdy (eds.), *Conformity and Conflict: Readings in Cultural Anthropology*, 4th ed. 1980 (Little, Brown, Boston, 1969), pp. 91–100.

43. Anthony Seeger, "The Meaning of Body Ornaments: A Suyá Example." *Ethnology*, vol. 14 (1975), pp. 211–24.

44. Gebhart-Sayer, op. cit., p. 4.

45. In Shipibo ideology contagion is likened to evil, swirling black clouds of spiritual "winds=emanations" or a tangled mass of dirty spider's webs.

46. E. Jean Langdon ("Siona Clothing and Adornment, or, You Are What You Wear," in Justine Cordwell and David Browman [eds.], *The Fabric of Culture: The Anthropology of Clothing & Adornment* [Mouton Publishers, The Hague, 1979], pp. 297–311) has demonstrated how the patterns in the facial paint and on painted textiles of the Siona-Secoya, an ethnic group from the Ecuadorian *montaña* to the north, emulate the positive designs of the *yagé* people of the celestial world above. These spirits derive their name from the visions produced by drinking a hallucinogenic tea rich in LSD-like alkaloids made from the vine *Banisteriopsis caapi*. In the same "transitive" manner the underworld beings emulate the sartorial art of the humans above them, whom they regard as their *yagé* people.

47. Dualism is always present in the "implicit mythology" of body decoration in South America. Just as the hut and surrounding village can be seen in profile or in overhead, plane-view, so too can the body reflect vertically stacked and concentric imagery. The vertical zones of a standing profile human figure are obvious: in descending order, bicep ligatures, breastplate, belt, bracelets, below-knee ligatures and anklets. But for the spirit's-eye plane-view one must imagine the body lying stretched out face-upward on the plaza, with arms and legs akimbo. In this view the innermost "ring" of corporeal art is the necklace of jaguar claws or teeth (ill. 20). The next ring out is the above-bicep arm ligatures and the breastplate, and the succeeding ring consists of the bracelets and the belt of jaguar skin, the below-knee ligatures and, lastly, the anklets. Thus, in a profile (vertical)-view, one's decorated body forms a stacked set of world levels, while in plane-view it inscribes a series of nested concentric rings of horizontal cosmic space; levels within levels, circles within circles.

48. Flutes, here "masculinized" by the addition of white feathers

from the male Sky World, are the principal tools of seduction. Men use them to serenade women in the evening and their tones are uniquely haunting; good flute players are thought to be particularly adept in their conquests. Since weapons, like the arrow which functions as a dance staff, must be held in the stronger right hand (the masculine hand), the flute must be grasped in the left (the feminine hand).

49. Cross-cultural anthropological studies show that societies which permit a close and intimate association between young boys and their mothers will construct horrific rites of passage to turn them into men while those which are characterized by a more tenuous association will adopt milder life crises rites for males. A psychological explanation that these ordeals serve to cut the apron strings forever is certainly supported by the Carib wasp-shield male puberty rite.

50. Amerindian dance is less noted for its showy or intricate choreography than for its continuous, slow shuffling, the steps being less an end in themselves than an approach to the spirits and a portal to a trancelike state where communication with them can occur. The music, too, is fairly simple in melodic structure, allowing the constant high, pure tones of the flutes and the rhythmic stamping of the feet and the rattles attached to them to aid in the attainment of altered consciousness.

51. In 1924 William Curtis Farabee (*The Central Caribs* [The University Museum, University of Pennsylvania, 1924], pp. 222–4) speculated that "sentimental reasons" might explain why ants were applied to certain parts of the body while wasps were applied to others. Here, our modern realization that the body is a cosmic map for lowlanders suggests an answer. The wasp is a winged insect, so it should be employed to attack the upper reaches of the somatic geography, specifically the chest and arms, while the ant, a terrestrial, crawling insect, should be applied to the lower regions, the buttocks, thighs and calves. My Wayana observations tend to confirm this dichotomy, again highlighting the importance of the positional code in performance analysis.

52. Gregor (1977, op. cit.) has already shown how this dramaturgical metaphor plays itself out in Mehinaku villages.

53. See Orlando and Claudio Villas Boas, *Xingu: The Indians, Their Myths* (Farrar, Straus & Giroux, New York, 1973), p. 159, for schematic drawings of the stylistic differences between the masks of water, land and tree spirits.

54. Ellen B. Basso, *A Musical View of the Universe: Kalapalo Myth and Ritual Performances* (University of Pennsylvania Press, Philadelphia, 1985), p. 246.

55. Ibid., p. 70.

56. Ibid., pp. 258–61.

57. Dennis Werner, *Amazon Journey: An Anthropologist's Year Among Brazil's Mekranoti Indians* (Prentice Hall, Englewood Cliffs, 1990), pp. 121–2.

58. David M. Guss, op. cit., pp. 35–9.

# Bibliography

Basso, Ellen B.
*A Musical View of the Universe: Kalapalo Myth and Ritual Performances.* University of Pennsylvania Press, Philadelphia, 1985.

Dwyer, Jane P. (ed.)
*The Cashinahua of Eastern Peru.* Studies in Anthropology and Material Culture 1. The Haffenreffer Museum of Anthropology, Brown University, Bristol, 1975.

Fock, Niels
*Waiwai: Religion and Society of an Amazonian Tribe.* Nationalmuseets Skrifter, Etnografisk Række (Ethnographic Series) 8. National Museum, Copenhagen, 1963.

Gebhart-Sayer, Angelika
*The Cosmos Encoiled: Indian Art of the Peruvian Amazon.* The Americas Society, New York, 1984.

Gerber, Peter R.
*Ka'apor: Menschen des Waldes und ihre Federkunst Eine bedrohte Kultur in Brasilien.* Völkerkunde-museum der Universitat Zurich, Zurich, 1991.

Gregor, Thomas
*Mehinaku: The Drama of Daily Life in a Brazilian Indian Village.* University of Chicago Press, Chicago, 1977.

Guss, David M.
*To Weave and To Sing: Art, Symbol, and Narrative In the South American Rain Forest.* The University of California Press, Berkeley and Los Angeles, 1989.

Hartmann, Gunther (ed.)
*Xingu: Unter Indianen in Zentral-Brasilien.* Sonderausstellung des Museums fir Völkerkunde, Dietrich Reimer Verlag, Berlin, 1986.

Hill, Jonathan D. (ed.)
*Rethinking History and Myth: Indigenous South American Perspectives on the Past.* University of Illinois Press, Urbana, 1988.

Lathrap, Donald W.
*The Upper Amazon.* Thames and Hudson, London, and Praeger, New York, 1970.

Lévi-Strauss, Claude
*Structural Anthropology.* Doubleday/Anchor Books, Garden City, 1967.

Meggers, Betty J.
*Amazonia: Man and Culture in a Counterfeit Paradise.* Aldine, Chicago, 1971.

Mekler, Adam.
*Invisible People: Art of the Amazon.* Fresno Art Museum, Fresno, California, 1992.

Reichel-Dolmatoff, Gerardo
*Beyond the Milky Way: Hallucinatory Imagery of the Tukano Indians.* UCLA Latin American Studies 42. University of California, UCLA Latin American Center, Los Angeles, 1978.

Reina, Ruben E. and Kenneth M. Kensinger (eds.)
*The Gift of Birds: Featherwork of Native South American Peoples.* University Museum Monograph 75. The University Museum of Archaeology and Anthropology, University of Pennsylvania, Philadelphia, 1991.

Roe, Peter G.
*The Cosmic Zygote: Cosmology in the Amazon Basin.* Rutgers University Press, New Brunswick, 1982.
"Of Rainbow Dragons and the Origins of Designs: The Waiwai *Urufiri* and the Shipibo *Ronin ëhua*." *Latin*

*American Indian Literatures Journal,* vol. 5, no. 1 (1989) pp. 1– 67.

"The Language of the Plumes: 'Implicit Mythology' in Shipibo, Cashinahua and Waiwai Feather Adornments," in Mary H. Preuss (ed.), *L.A.I.L. Speaks! Selected Papers From the Seventh International Symposium, Albuquerque, 1989.* Labyrinthos Press, Culver City, pp. 105–36, pls. A–F, 1990.

Roosevelt, Anna Curtenius
*Moundbuilders of the Amazon: Geophysical Archaeology on Marajó Island, Brazil.* Academic Press, New York, 1991.

Schoepf, Daniel
*L'art de la plume brésil.* Musée d'Ethnographie, Geneva, 1985.

Seeger, Anthony
"The Meaning of Body Ornaments: A Suyá Example." *Ethnology,* vol. 14 (1975) pp. 211–24.

Turner, Terrence
"Cosmetics: The Language of Bodily Adornment," in James P. Spradley and David W. McCurdy (eds.), *Conformity and Conflict: Readings in Cultural Anthropology.* 4th ed. Little, Brown, Boston, 1980 (First ed., 1969), pp. 91–100.

Urban, Greg and Janet Wall Hendricks
"Signal Functions of Masking in Amerindian Brazil." *Semiotica,* vol. 47, nos. 1–4 (1983) pp. 181–216.

Verswijver, Gustaaf (ed.)
*Kaiapo: Amazonia, the Art of Body Decoration.* Royal Museum for Central Africa, Tervuren, 1992.

Wagley, Charles
*Welcome of Tears: The Tapirapé Indians of Central Brazil.* Oxford University Press, New York, 1977.

Werner, Dennis
*Amazon Journey: An Anthropologist's Year Among Brazil's Mekranoti Indians.* Prentice Hall, Englewood Cliffs, 1990.

Whitten, Dorothea S. and Norman E. Whitten, Jr.
*From Myth to Creation: Art From Amazonian Ecuador.* University of Illinois Press, Urbana, 1988.

Wilbert, Johannes
"Warao Cosmology and Yekuana Roundhouse Symbolism." *Journal of Latin American Lore,* vol. 7, no. 1 (1981) pp. 37–72.

Yde, Jens
*Material Culture of the Waiwai.* Nationalmuseets Skrifter, Etnografisk Række (Ethnographic Series) 10. National Museum of Denmark, Copenhagen, 1965.

## Acknowledgments for illustrations

James Marshall, Collection of the Bowers Museum of Cultural Art, 11, 29, 56, 57, 74, 87, 88 (1955–60); Russell A. Mittermeier, 1, 12, 26 (1991–2); Peter G. Roe, 7; E.Z. Smith, Fresno, California, All photographs of objects.